# THE
# SYNERGY
# GAME

## GEORGIA CLARE

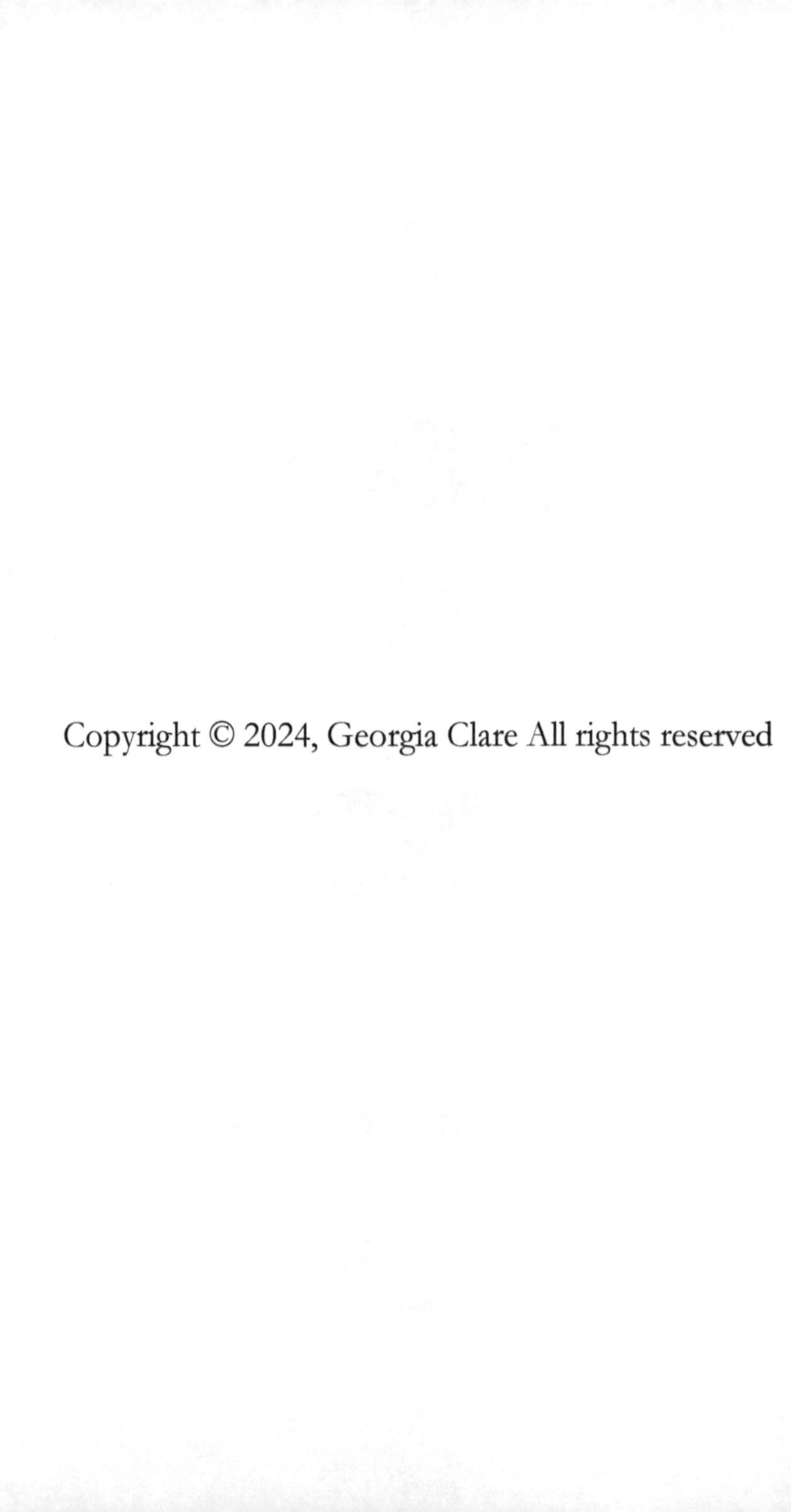

To Candace and Lara, the
motivation and inspiration for
everything I do, and to Robert who
helped me see the books inside me,
who showed me how to dream the
impossible and who helped me
discover myself and my purpose.

# CONTENTS

# INTRODUCTION

What do you do when you feel like you don't want to live, you have lost everything that you lived for, and you can't seem to find even the smallest sliver of joy? When the days are endless and grey, and you can barely summon up the energy or the inclination to get out of bed. When you feel so lost you don't think you will ever be able to find yourself ever again.

You stop.

You remember.

You dig deeper than you ever thought you could.

You find a reason. There is always one if you look hard enough.

There was a distant thought in the back of my mind, so distant that I could barely hear it. But it said *what if?* What if I gave up and I missed out on being happy again. What if I could have a future? Even though I didn't see how or if that could happen, there was the nagging feeling in those far away corners of my mind that had that little thought. What if?

What if I could survive this?

That little thought became a constant drone in my head. I'd survived before, nothing as huge as this, but maybe I could. I gave myself a few more days to wallow, un-showered, hiding at home between my bed and the sofa, not caring if I ate or not, drank or not. I decided that Monday I would rise again. Monday would be the day when I gave living another shot.

Monday came around, and I showered and made myself a list (I'm a big fan of lists!). Shower, get dressed, drink tea, write, meditate, eat, and walk in the forest. Each time I did something on my list, I'd cross it off, feeling quite a sense of accomplishment. I did this every day for weeks and weeks, adding more things to the list as I got stronger.

So many things helped me to survive the worst year of my life, the year my marriage to my best friend and soulmate broke up, the year I never would have imagined I could survive. This book is a compilation of all those things, how I did them, how they helped and what I still use now. I learned so much that year. I learned who I was, deep down, discovering myself for the first time in my life. I learned that I was a lot stronger than I ever imagined I could be. I learned what I needed in my life and what I could live without, not what I thought it would be. We think we know ourselves, but until we have been brought to rock bottom, have been through something that devastates us and must decide whether we want to give up completely or rise from the ashes, we are coasting through life. It may be a good life, a relatively happy life, but deep down, do we really know ourselves? I found out that I didn't. I had spent most of my life making sure I made other people happy. I thought that was how to make myself happy. But when I lost the only constant and steady thing in my life, I was adrift and at sea without direction or purpose. I didn't know which way to turn or what to do. I had a panicky feeling that I had never felt before and thankfully never have since. The worst thing I could ever imagine happening had happened, and I could barely breathe, never mind think. But at the back of my mind were those two words – what if.

I realised that if I could survive this, I might help others to do the same, to survive what seems impossible, to survive what you are not even sure you want to survive. I've come through this with so much determination to rebuild my life even better than it was before, and I want to share my journey with you. I realised in the middle of it all how much comfort I got from other people's words. To feel that there was someone out there who understood made a huge difference. That's why I'm writing this book. When we feel most alone, we need to know that we are heard, understood and supported. It makes all the difference. What I found is that when you have sunk even further than rock bottom and when the light at the end of the tunnel is not there, it's the little things that matter that make the difference. Lots of little things all put together. That's what gets you through.

This is how I did it.

# CHAPTER ONE
# WRITING TO HEAL

---

*Scribbling My Way to Sanity*

*"I write because I don't know what I
think until I read what I say."*

Flannery O'Connor

I think writing literally saved my sanity. When I really thought I was losing it, when the questions just wouldn't stop whizzing around in my head, I would write about it. By writing, I would make sense of things, of my world that bore no resemblance to any world I'd ever been in before.

Let me just back up a bit, though, and tell you how I got into the writing habit. Yes, it is a habit, and like anything good for us, it must become a part of what we do, who we are, a habit. When I was a child, I always kept a journal and wrote endless stories. Then, as life got busier, marriage, children and work, I stopped writing. Well, not completely, but I wrote sporadically. A few years ago I started to learn more about spirituality and how it related. I learned about gratitude, and the suggestion was to write a gratitude journal. So I did. It seemed like a great thing to do; I had a lot to be grateful for, and I could see the value in reminding myself of that every day.

I researched as I always do when starting something new, and read somewhere you should get yourself a journal that you look forward to writing in. I'm tactile and visual, so I liked the idea of Moleskine notebooks as they feel nice and come in pretty colours! I now have a cupboard full of them, like a rainbow of the last ten years of my life.

At first I would list ten things I was grateful for right then, in that moment. Sometimes, I wrote the same things every day. Gradually, though, my mindset changed. I didn't need to force being grateful, I just was. It was literally changing me, this simple habit. I have never been a negative person, but I tended to worry and dwell on issues. A side effect of dwelling on all the things I was grateful for, was that I became someone who always had a smile on her face. It gave me confidence in what I could do because I was always thinking about how much I already had. Then it just became who I am, my paradigm, and I didn't need to write about it anymore, I lived it.

But I still wanted to write, and the timing was not a coincidence either. I thought I would write about my life, or more accurately, my feelings about my life. I was in my early fifties, and things were rather challenging. I'd had issues with my family, who were not happy about the direction my life had taken and some choices I'd made, and so had decided to cut me off and not talk to me. (I'd left a religion that I'd been part of my whole life as I didn't agree with the policies.) Those family members were my mother and my brother, so it was traumatic to deal with their rejection and shunning.

I started to pour my hurt and sadness out into the pages of my journal, and the effects were amazing. First, it was getting it all out of me, releasing it from my mind and body. It was like a therapy. The second benefit was that I often wrote things down on paper before I'd understood them in my mind, hence the quote at the beginning of this chapter. I didn't always think about what I wrote, so I was accessing my subconscious and finding out how I felt about things. I kept reminding myself that this was for me, no one else would read it. That meant I could be honest and pour my heart out.

This turned out to be excellent practice for what came next when writing each day became my lifeline. When I had to let go of what was inside before I exploded. I had spent two years writing about what was going wrong with my marriage, how frustrated I was feeling, and how it felt to suddenly seem invisible, to feel old and unwanted. It was through writing that I realised what I had to do. It was by putting my jumbled-up thoughts down on paper I saw what my logical thinking mind would not let me see. I saw that I was losing myself, losing my dignity and finally seeing what I hadn't wanted to see, everything had changed.

So I left to come back to see my daughter in France. I came back to our home here, and two weeks later, my deepest fears were realised, and my world fell apart. I finally faced what I'd known for some time in my subconscious, what had been making me sick for the last two years, the chronic stress and stomach problems that I'd put down to menopause. I found out my husband was having an affair. It's as if the distance (he was in Asia) had given me the clarity I needed to see what was so obvious once I'd seen it. We were talking on FaceTime, and I just knew. Desperate this time for the truth, I just couldn't take it anymore, I begged for honesty. My intuition, sharpened by reflections penned over the past two weeks, had already revealed what I sensed to be undeniable.

I don't think I've ever needed my writing practice as I did in those next few days, weeks and months as he turned into, or rather I was seeing, the man that I had loved for over thirty-four years had disappeared and in his place was someone I didn't know. I was more scared than I'd ever been in my life before. It was a suffocating fear that I had never felt before. As if I was lost at sea, all alone and certain I would die, there was no help. I was suddenly faced with a life I didn't know how to live, a house I didn't know how to fix (we were 2/3 of the way through a renovation) and a car that I had never taken to a garage or had to maintain.

So I wrote about all my fears and my sadness and pain and devastation, and as the weeks turned into months, I made sense of things that made no sense. I saw beyond what I was feeling. My writing gave me clarity and helped me make decisions. It was while I was writing one day, on our thirty-third wedding anniversary, one of the saddest days of my life, that it came to me that I wanted a divorce. There was no fixing things. He wouldn't even speak to me, plus what kind of life would it be for either of us if we got back together? He's late home one day and what am I instantly going to think?!

No, it was over, and I wanted closure and to take control. I didn't file for divorce straight away. I wasn't strong enough for that, but I'd made the decision.

Over the next months, as I wrote, I got stronger. It's like I understood myself better. When my marriage ended, I didn't know who I was. Who am I if I'm not his wife, his partner, his friend? We had been together for so long that I wasn't even sure of my likes and dislikes anymore. I don't mean I acquiesced to all his wishes; our relationship wasn't like that. For so long, we were best friends and lovers. But my identity was all wrapped up in him. We did everything together, worked together, travelled together and had fun together until we didn't. So, to actually figure out what I liked, just me, not considering anyone else, was tough.

I remember being in the supermarket one day, and I was putting the usual stuff in the cart, and I suddenly thought, hang on, do I even like this food? I had to relearn all over again who I was as just me. What clothes did I like to wear, what did I like to drink, what did I want my house to look like, and the big, huge one, what the fuck do I want to do with the rest of my life? Guess what helped? Writing! I wrote about how I felt about all the newness, which was now starting to feel like freedom. And the more I wrote about it the more I found out who I was and who I wanted to be.

One day, as I was writing, I wrote about how nice it was not to have to think about what someone else thought of how you looked. I'd tried everything for the previous year to get him to notice me: new clothes, new lingerie, new hairstyle. It was such a relief to look in the mirror and think yes, I look good for me. I like the way I look, and I don't need to wonder if anyone else likes what I'm wearing today or how I've styled my hair. It was one of those times when my writing told me how I was feeling. Like Flannery O'Connor said, "I write because I don't know what I think until I read what I say." When I first read that quote, it was like a hug from a close friend. Someone had put into words exactly what was happening when I wrote. It was another one of those times when I felt heard and seen and understood, a connection.

As I entered the dating world after a very long absence, writing helped me to figure out what I wanted in a man. I'd never thought of it before. I fell in love with my husband in my late teens, I didn't think too deeply about it! He was my friend, we fell in love, we had lots of fun, and we liked the same things. He was also very good-looking and dressed nicely. All things that are so important when you are in your teens! But now, what was I even looking for? I realised I didn't have a clue. I listed all the qualities I wanted in an ideal man. I took quite a while to make the list and I surprised myself with what I came up with. Things like I want him to be kind, thoughtful and generous, not just to me but to other people. I want him to be healthy, something I'd never considered before, but at my age, many people haven't taken care of their health, and when you get to your 50s, it starts to show. I wrote that I wanted someone who was a good communicator as that was one of the factors in the breakdown of my marriage, maybe of all marriages. And I wanted someone with some of the same interests as me so we could, above all, be best friends and not just lovers.

When I went on dates, I wrote about it after. I wrote about the attention I was getting and how it made me feel. I liked being seen again. I liked feeling like a pretty woman again instead of a middle-aged invisible wife. I wrote about the possibility of falling in love again and how it terrified me, and then I wrote about my not being ready to date. As fun as all the attention was, I needed to be me for a while. I needed to finish discovering who I was before I could give my full attention to someone else. And so, for the first time in my life, I became truly single.

I started to write about the incredible freedom I had for the first time in my life. How it wasn't as scary as I thought it would be, but it was so very liberating. My childhood experiences of sexual abuse made sure I was aware of boys from a young age. My first crush was when I was about five or six on a boy at school, and it never stopped. There was always someone I was in love with, and then I got married at twenty. So, to be completely man-free was a new experience and one I desperately needed for my growth. Through my daily journalling, I realised that I was enjoying the freedom of not looking for a date or waiting for someone to text me back or call me. For the first time in my life, I was just me.

And that's when I started to write this book!

*There are many writing resources on my website georgiaclare.com. Tips on how to start and what to write when you decide to journal, ideas and prompts to get you started.

# CHAPTER TWO
# EMBRACING GRATITUDE

---

*From Daily Ritual to Lifeline*

*"Be grateful for what you already have while you pursue your goals. If you aren't grateful for what you already have, what makes you think you would be happy with more?"*

Roy T Bennett

I first read about the idea of practicing gratitude many years ago. I knew about being grateful and that my life was pretty good compared to many. I'd travelled enough to see that. But actually making it a daily practice, something that I was conscious of doing, that was new. I thought it was a good idea, so I started keeping a gratitude journal. I would write ten things every day I was grateful for. It wasn't hard at the time, as my life was running pretty smoothly.

I started writing in Moleskine journals, just a page a day for a while. Sometimes, I would even write the same or similar things each day. It didn't matter, as writing was helping impress on my mind what I was grateful for. It reminded me each day of my blessings.

It had a few benefits. As I always did it first thing in the morning while I was drinking my tea, it was a good start to the day. It's difficult to have a bad day when you've started off thinking about how many great things you have in your life.

Secondly as this became my regular practice, I found I was noticing more things to be grateful for. I was becoming more mindful, more observant. So, I wasn't just showing gratitude for those ten things I'd written in the morning, I was noticing things throughout my day to be grateful for as well.

It wasn't hard at first. That's why you should never delay starting this practice. Because it's good to be in that habit if things become challenging, which happened to me. A couple of years after I started doing this, I made a major life change. I left the strict religious group I had been a part of for my whole life. Why I did it is irrelevant here, but the consequences of doing it meant that my former friends no longer wanted contact with me. My mother and my brother also cut off all contact and wanted nothing more to do with me.

Suddenly, I needed to find ten things to be grateful for every single day. I needed to focus on the good in my life so the pain of all the rejection didn't overwhelm me. The rejection by my mother was the hardest to take. That broke my heart. I have two children and I spent countless hours trying to imagine what they could do that would make me want to never speak to them again. I couldn't think of anything. I imagined the worst crimes they could commit or the most horrid things they could do, and I would still want to be in their lives. I would still love them. I'm their mother FFS! So, not comprehending why my own mother would follow some manmade rules and put that first rather than me, her daughter, still to this day is something I will never understand. It hurt, it hurt so much.

Another thing about writing a gratitude list is that you won't believe how good it makes you feel. Focusing on what you have, instead of what you don't have, what you're missing, is an absolute life changer. We can always find things lacking in our life. Maybe we want more money, more friends, a better job, better health, romance, adventure etc. etc. But the amazing thing is that once you start to focus on what you have, you seem to attract more of it. So, you focus on how that one friend you have is so special to you and how grateful you are to have her in your life and guess what? You attract more friends like that.

It's not magic. It's the law of attraction or, more accurately, the law of vibration. It's the way things work. The universe gives us more of how we feel. So, if we feel happy and grateful, we attract more things to be happy and grateful about. If we feel unhappy and that we lack in any way, guess what will happen? The universe responds to our vibe. It reminds me of a bible verse in Matthew 'For to everyone who has, more will be given, and he will have abundance; but from him who does not have, even what he has will be taken away.'

I always used to think it was cruel and miserable for God to do that, but now I realise it has nothing to do with a god. It's we who determine what we have and what we don't have. It makes total sense now. So, if our feelings and thoughts determine our lives, shouldn't we make sure that they are good thoughts and feelings? The best way to do that is to live with gratitude to make it a daily practice.

Focusing each day on my blessings, no matter how bad I was feeling set me up for my biggest challenge to come a couple of years later. This was when my marriage broke up, and my fairy tale life came to a screeching halt and turned into a drama with a sad ending. This is when my gratitude practice changed from 'Things I have to be grateful for' to 'Things I have to live for'. I had to dig so deeply to find my blessings, to find things to be grateful for because it seemed as if there was nothing. But the more I wrote, the more I realised that it was the little things and maybe some things I had taken for granted when my life was going so well.

I had my daughters and my sister; I had friends. I was beyond grateful for them, but my world had fallen apart, and I needed to find reasons to want to see the spring and another birthday. So, I started back at the beginning. My morning cup of tea, hearing the birds singing in the tree outside my window, a warm fire, a house I felt safe in, living in a beautiful village with good neighbours, a reliable car to drive (a necessity, as where I live is rural), the light on the trees in the evening, a stray cat that seemed to come and check up on me every day (my daughter named him Mr. Tuna, but that's another story!) and on and on. I looked for small things because the big things had gone. And in the small things, I found peace, and it made me stop and realise that although I felt that I had lost everything, I still had so much.

I didn't write lists any more. I wrote pages of how much help I was getting, how my sister messaged me every single day to make sure I was ok, how my youngest daughter went shopping for me when I couldn't bring myself to leave the house and how much her little gifts in the following weeks meant, my eldest daughter calling me every day those first few weeks with her sweet love and understanding, how amazing my neighbours were in looking after me, how I just seemed to be gathering more friends around me and how comforting their support was, how grateful I was for the forest at the back of my house so I could walk in nature and feel that strength and how grateful I was to feel safe in my home.

Then, I started to be grateful for my strength, my determination and my courage. I wouldn't have realised this if I hadn't been in the habit of writing each day and looking for things to be grateful for. Doing this saved my sanity in those first few months; it saved my dignity and my grace so I wasn't tempted to indulge in revenge or 'pay back'. (Well, I must admit, I burned his favourite hat on the fire!) But I realised how grateful I was for all the things I'd learned, all the tools I had at my disposal, and in realising that, I started to use them all.

I used my knowledge of herbs and nutrition to keep myself healthy though the winter, as it was my first cold winter in many years. Previously we had spent all our winters in Thailand. I started to listen to music all the time and to dance when I felt happy and when I felt sad. I meditated every day and connected to a place outside of myself, a higher power, a wisdom, I listened within to get through the days. I used crystals and reiki, yoga, positive reminders everywhere. All these things and more were practices

I'd learned mostly over the past 6 to 8 years. It was as if the universe was preparing me for the biggest challenge of my life. When it came, I won't say I was prepared, but I had the tools to get me through it. And once I realised that I knew I could do it, I knew I could survive. And I was more grateful than I'd ever been in my life before because I knew now that I wanted to do it. I wanted to survive. I knew how. I would just be grateful for one day at a time and remember how many blessings I still had, even though I'd lost the person I thought I couldn't live without and with that, everything I thought I could count on in my life.

What I discovered, though, is that I can't live without me, and I can always count on me. I became grateful for myself. I learned new ways to practice gratitude so it became something that was a part of me and a part of who I was becoming. I took gratitude walks. As I walked through the forest, whether it was an energetic walk up the hill or a stroll through the trees and by the river, with every step I would say thank you. After every thank you, I would think of something I was grateful for. It's amazing how many things you can think of to say thank you for when you don't think too much. You walk and say thank you, and things pop into your mind, and the realisation hits that, wow, there is so much I'm grateful for. I would come home from those walks not only energised by being out in nature, in the forest, but also with a heart full of gratitude. A surprising effect of doing that was the feeling of connection I would get. It seemed to connect me with everything in my life, everything around me. I was grateful for so many people in my life, the things I had materially, the beauty around me and the support of the unseen forces I could feel around me.

Another practice I adopted was making a gratitude jar. Every night before I go to bed, I write on a small piece of paper the one thing I am most grateful for that day. It focused my mind for a few moments as I ran though my day, and looked for all the happy moments, and chose the best one. Sometimes it was a hug from my daughter, or talking to my other daughter via video, the feeling of solitude as I wrote in the morning, the feeling of peace and acceptance, a sweet message from a friend or something I'd accomplished that I was proud of.

But there was something else apart from writing and being grateful that was to get me though those dark days of my winter, and it's something I still do every day now.

# CHAPTER THREE
# MY JOURNEY TO STILLNESS

---

*How Meditation Became My
Sanctuary and Guide*

*"Be still. Stillness reveals the secrets of
eternity"*

Lao Tzu

Meditation saved me from going mad and losing my mind completely.

That sounds dramatic, but it's what happened.

There's already been so much written, videoed and said about meditation. So what I will talk about here is particularly how it helped me and the exact journey I've taken to learn to make my meditation a practice that I do daily and is a part of my life.

I started meditating as a regular practice in 2018. At first, I went onto YouTube and looked for guided meditations because that seemed the easiest way to start.  I started with some positive type meditations, some that would help me to move on from the big change I'd made in my life and the consequences of the decision that I'd made. Meditation would help me navigate these changes. I'd heard a lot about the benefits. The benefits of being still, the benefits of sitting and going within. But for me, this had to be learned. I was the sort of person that was always occupied. I didn't generally sit and do nothing. I had a book, or I was doing something with my hands, I've always been creative with knitting, sewing, drawing, painting, an art project, or watching TV, and even then, I would often sit with some knitting or jewellery making pieces while watching, so I wasn't used to sitting and doing nothing.

At first, the guided meditations helped me because I knew how long they would take, and it kept my mind focused. It was training my mind, and it was training my brain to be focused on one thing. On my website, I have guided meditations that I've created, and I've listed some of my favourite YouTube meditation channels that really helped me when I started this journey.

The second stage of my meditation journey was that I got to where the guided meditations had served their purpose, and I now concentrated and focused more, so the next progress in my meditation journey was to listen to some music. (Again, on my website on the music page, I have beautiful playlists I have curated that you can use for meditation.) I would sit with music, and I think at first I would sit for maybe ten minutes, but then gradually it went up to between twenty and thirty minutes. Now I usually meditate for around thirty minutes, sometimes less, sometimes more, depending on what's going on in my life and what I need.

One thing that helped me a couple of years

ago was that I went on a meditation course when I was living in Thailand. The course was in Bangkok, and it was a ten-day course to help develop psychic awareness through, over the ten days, a series of twenty-five meditations. It was actually one of the hardest things I've ever done because sitting for that long looking within made me face pretty deep things, childhood trauma, how I really felt about my parents, my relationship with my husband that was coming to an end, although I didn't know it consciously and I also learned a lot about myself and how I viewed things. It not only deepened my meditation practice, but it also taught me how to go deeper in meditation and how to connect better with spirit, with my guides. It was probably one of the best courses I've ever done, and I've done a few. I learned how to get into a deeper meditative state. There are different brainwave states. According to clarkebioscience.com, "Alpha brainwaves relate to creativity and daydreaming, Beta waves are produced in the middle of deep thinking, Delta/Theta waves can be found during deep sleep, and Gamma waves are associated with problem-solving, happiness, and compassion." The deeper we can go the more we can access our sub conscious and stop our thinking logical brain. This gives us access to a higher self, purer thoughts and basically, what is best for us. And not what we think is best for us, but what is actually best for us, for our soul, our purpose and our path. This is where we manifest, heal and find answers to problems.

Once I moved back to France, I mediated without music, in stillness. I live in a quiet place, and I live alone, so there are no noises I need to block out. I can sit in my yoga room on my meditation cushion and be still, silent, and listening.

This is when my meditation became even more a part of who I am. It's my time when I connect and go within and check with my higher self to see if what is going on in my life is ok. If it's not to see how I can fix it. If there are things I don't understand, I can either gain wisdom and understanding or get to a place where I can accept that it is not in my best interests to know or to find out. It is best for me to trust I will get the knowledge when it's the right time for me.

For example, this morning, I wanted to understand why I hadn't been sleeping properly. I knew if I was still enough and humble enough to listen, I would get the answer. I often get in my own way as I like to fix things. I like answers, and I don't like waiting long for the answers to come. Meditation has humbled me, and I've realised that I don't always have the answers, and I can't always fix everything that I want to, that sometimes it's best to let things break, and it's actually better for me in the long run. So, I sat quietly this morning and asked why I was feeling anxious and not sleeping well. The answer I got was that I was finding it hard to let go at a deeper level and that it was time for me to think about forgiveness. More on that in a later chapter.

It's like Aristotle said, "Knowing yourself is the beginning of all wisdom". Meditation helped me to see beyond what I actually knew, what I could see, helped me see what was invisible to my physical eyes, and to know myself deeply, to see inside. It shut off my logical thinking and allowed my higher self to take over. This way, I could get answers and gain insights into things going on that my stressed-out and devastated mind could not process. I didn't know how to live or exist when my marriage broke up. To think of everything I now had to do by myself, learn how to do it, and the simple act of living on my own when I had been part of a couple for almost thirty-four of my fifty-three years seemed like an impossible task.

In meditation, I got strength and a respite from my mind, which was whirling non-stop with questions and what-ifs. For those 30 minutes a day, there was quiet, there was calm, there was a semblance of peace. In meditation, I was able to gain clarity, step away from the situation and look at it from a different perspective. Every day I would ask for guidance from my higher self, from Spirit. All I asked for was to be shown what was best for me. How I could best live. And each day I came away from my meditation with just enough strength to face that day. Until it got better and better, and I got stronger and stronger, knowing that if there was something I didn't understand or that I had to decide on, I could sit for a while and let the answer come.

I started using my meditation practice to visualise, too. To imagine the life I wanted to live again, the things I wanted to accomplish. When my mind is still, I can do this and it gives me direction and clarity for the way I want to go, for how I want my day to look. Doing this gave my days focus. Instead of wandering day to day, getting through the week, the month and the year, I set goals and used my meditation time to see them done and accomplished. It changed my mindset and is what I do now and one of the ways I have rebuilt my life to succeed in every way.

Now meditation is a practice I do daily that is part of my routine. It's how I have come to terms with the loss in my life, the injustice and the cruelty, because I've discovered something that made all the difference. We are all connected. I'm not separate. I'm not alone. I'm protected and guided. I'm connected to every other living thing and that all the wisdom, all the answers I need are there for me if I listen.

My meditation practice now has changed quite a lot from when I started. It's even changed from a year ago. I've realised it grows with you. It gives you what you need. At one time, I needed peace and respite from my pain, now, I need to still my busy mind and find balance each day. My life is busy with the new path I have taken, new ideas and projects I'm working on. I use part of my meditation practice now to visualise how I want things to unfold in my personal and professional life. If I have questions, I ask, and when I am able to be still and listen, I get the answers. Not always the ones I'm expecting, but always ones that are best for me and my purpose, my goals. Sometimes, I sit in silence, and sometimes, I use an app with binaural meditation music.

It's amazing how things go together and how the next tool I use fits perfectly with my meditation practice. All the learning how to be still and focus prepared me for the next practice I would learn was essential to my healing journey. The synergy was falling into place.

# CHAPTER FOUR
# YOGA: MY PATH TO STRENGTH

---

*Finding My Power, Peace, and*
*Purpose on the Mat*

*"Yoga does not just change the way we*
*see things, it transforms the person who*
*sees."*

B.K.S. Iyengar

I've done yoga on and off for many years. I went to a class for a few weeks in Florida. I spent 6 months going to a hot yoga class in Thailand three times a week. It wasn't until I came back to France that I became obsessed with it. My friend is a yoga teacher and has her own beautiful yoga studio. She also does retreats, but I am lucky enough to live just two minutes' drive from her, so I can go anytime.

When she found out that I was back to stay, not just for my usual five or six months and that the reason for that was that I'd left my husband, one thing she suggested was that I come to her classes twice a week. Actually, she didn't suggest it. She told me I needed it! And she was right. She explained that the reason she got into yoga over twenty years ago was that she was at a difficult period in her life, a traumatic period. She told me that yoga saved her mind and body, and that she thought it would do the same for me. She said it would be a time when I wouldn't have to think of anything else but yoga. A mind break.

So I started going on a Monday and a Friday morning. Her class was an hour and a half, and it was a nice social time as other friends went and I made new friends too. There were six of us regularly at those classes during that long winter. Those women became my strength and my rock. They hugged me, loved me and encouraged me. I made a promise to myself that no matter what the weather I would be there at nine am on those mornings, week in, week out. That may not sound like much, but for me, it was my first winter in Europe in about seven years. The thought of going out when there was frost on my windscreen horrified me, but something inside me knew Sam was right. I needed this. Not just the company and support of the other women, but I needed the yoga itself.

The other yoga classes I went to were purely for the exercise benefit. This class, however, was different. It was taught by someone who really understood the body and anatomy and, more importantly, the mind-body connection. At first, I was wobbly and stiff, and I took a while to learn the poses. I was taught the importance of breathing correctly. For someone who has had asthma all her life, I've never taken breathing for granted. Now, however, I was learning the power of the breath, how breathing correctly gives you strength to go deeper into the pose and hold it for longer.

I went to the class twice a week all through that

very long winter, never missing any, apart from one week when I had a cold. I gradually went from thinking it was good for me physically to realising that it was benefiting me mentally, too. As I learned the poses and I didn't have to concentrate on that so much, I focused more. I blocked other things out and focused on feeling the stretch where I should be feeling it, on breathing when I should and how I should, and I started to only think about what I was doing, nothing else. I became absorbed in what I was doing, and my mind rested. For an hour and a half, I entered a different world, a world of movement and breathing, pushing my body and learning to appreciate what it could do. For those first few months, it was an escape from the pain and sadness of my days.

By the start of summer, when Sam stopped her weekly classes to run her retreats, I felt I knew enough to practice on my own. She had been careful to teach us how to do the poses safely so we wouldn't injure ourselves and I felt confident that I could do it myself. At first, I planned on keeping to the two days a week, but one day, in casual conversation, Sam said something to me that would change everything. She said, "You won't believe how strong your body becomes when you do yoga every day". You know that feeling you get when something, an inner voice, says to you, DO IT! I knew this was what I needed to do.

I have to explain something here. I've never been enthusiastic about exercise. I've had asthma all my life, and as a child, I was ill and not able to join in with sports at school. Exercise was never encouraged at home. Reading, study and crafts were, but not sport! So I grew up doing the minimum required at school and never having any sports as hobbies. I lived in the country, in Wales, so I did a lot of walking and hiking when my asthma permitted. Even when my chest issues improved as an adult, I only did things sporadically, not seeing the need for it. I never had a weight problem and considered myself fit enough. However, I always knew at the back of my mind that exercise was important and that I needed to add it to my routine somehow. So, I would start yoga classes or a gym membership, only to give up after a few months. Nothing ever lasted. Until Sam's classes!

I don't know what it was or how I became addicted. Maybe it was the right time in my life. That I now had the freedom to only consider myself. Maybe it was my subconscious screaming at me that I needed it. Maybe it was Sam's enthusiasm and excellent teaching. Whatever it was, I suddenly realised I wanted to know what it felt like to have a strong body and to be fit. I wanted to see how far I could go with this, how much my body could do at fifty-four. I'd already bought a yoga mat, so I added a fancy yoga towel, too. You know one of those that are the same shape and size as the mat? I felt like a real yogi!

At the back of my house, there is a long room with windows all along. At one time, it was a balcony, but a previous owner had boxed it all in and made it into a beautifully bright room. I realised that it was the perfect place to practice. It looked out onto my garden and is not overlooked. I decided to see if I could do it every day during the week, five days, Monday to Friday. I found that as much as I loved the classes I loved even more doing it on my own. I could focus without distractions, I could get immersed in the yoga flow. And that was great until the start of winter when it got too cold. That part of the house takes time to warm up, and as I had been taught it's dangerous to exercise when you are cold, I made my own yoga room from a spare bedroom upstairs. It was a room I'd used for meditation and some Reiki and crystal healing I did for a while. It was the perfect space. Easy to heat and easy to keep the energy high. It's where I practice today. Surrounded by my beautiful crystals, it has become my sacred space.

Coming from a childhood of sexual abuse, I had never had a great relationship with my body. I didn't want to see it or I wasn't happy about something when I saw it. I often felt I was overweight somewhere, even though I can see now I never was. I would look critically at my thighs, which were too large, or my stomach, which wasn't flat enough, saggy breasts, wrinkles. The older I grew, this only became worse, especially when my husband stopped 'seeing' me. I thought there must be something wrong with my body. That must be why he doesn't want me anymore.

The thing with yoga is that you have to look at yourself a lot while you are doing it to do it correctly. Ideally there needs to be a mirror so you can check your alignment. This isn't for vanity but to make sure you are holding the pose correctly, if not, you can easily injure yourself. So for the first time in my life, I was seeing myself differently. I was seeing what my body could do, how far I could push it, and most importantly, how it was changing. I'd never looked at myself so much before. I started to like what I saw, I was falling in love with myself. I still noticed things that were not perfect, but now that stomach that wasn't perfectly flat, I saw as a stomach that had carried my two beautiful daughters. Those thighs that were not as firm and perfect as I'd like were thighs they had sat on when I was reading stories to them. Those saggy breasts fed them. Those wrinkles are a story of my life. They are from when I was worried when they were sick, from laughing and smiling at the wonder of them. My body is the story of my life, and there is nothing I am ashamed of anymore. It took me looking at myself in the mirror for an hour and a half daily for me to see that, for me to realise that I'm enough as I am. I'm perfect as me.

I'm perfect in my imperfection.

I saw that actually, I wasn't an old, middle-aged, washed-up woman. I was actually not bad looking, in pretty good shape, and it wasn't that I was lacking in some way that my marriage had broken down. It wasn't me. I finally acknowledged that it wasn't my fault. Whatever issues my husband had that made him act the way he did, treat me the way he did, they were not for me to worry about now. It was his problem, not mine.

It's amazing how my life has changed since I started yoga. Sam was right. I am amazed at how strong I am. Physically but also mentally and emotionally too. Because it requires this focus, it seems to let thoughts and ideas come up, to just pop into your head from nowhere. I've had times where I have just, out of nowhere, burst out crying or sunk to the floor, howling and releasing a deep sadness. It's as if once my focus is elsewhere, I've been able to release what needs to be let go of. For me, this could only have happened in a solitary practice. I couldn't have ever let myself go in a class with other people, even though most are my friends. I'm at the point now where I couldn't imagine my life without my yoga practice. I know it keeps me fit physically and tones and strengthens my body, which I like. The addictive thing, though, is the absolute focus and dedication I feel once I go into my yoga room and shut the door. I meditate on my cushion for about twenty minutes, then I put on my favourite chilled music playlist, sit on my mat and enter another world.

I use it as a healing tool, but it has such far-reaching benefits it will be part of my life until I take my last breath.

And speaking of music, that's a tool I had all

along but never realised how I could use it as one. Once I did, the power of it amazed me.

# CHAPTER FIVE
# THE HEALING POWER OF MUSIC

---

*Transforming Trauma and Embracing
Self-Love Through Sound*

*"Music expresses that which cannot be
put into words and that cannot remain
silent"*

Victor Hugo

I've always loved music. Growing up there was always music playing, either the radio or a record. It's always been a big part of my life, but it's only recently that I've viewed it as a healing tool.

When I first became interested in energy medicine and started studying it, I came across quite a lot of information about how different music frequencies or vibrations can affect us. Imagine for a minute how you feel after listening to a beautiful piece of classical music as opposed to a piece of heavy rock music. It all has to do with the frequency. Now, there is nothing wrong with listening to rock music. I love dance music especially when I'm cleaning my house! But here I will separate the two types of music, one being music that makes me feel good and the other being music proven to be healing.

I listen to a lot of music, and my tastes are eclectic. I found I could use music to change my mood or to release emotion. On days I was feeling down, I would choose my music carefully. I needed music that would either uplift me and remind me how beautiful life is, such as a beautiful classical piece, or something to get me energised, something with a good beat and empowering lyrics. If I felt down while listening to a certain song or piece of music, I would make myself change it to something that would change my vibration and my feelings.

For a long time after I separated from my husband, there seemed to be a lot of music that was hard to listen to. Music had featured in our home together a lot and we loved going to concerts of all types together. So many songs either reminded me of him or the lyrics reminded me of what had ended, what I'd lost. Then, one day, I had a brainwave! I was listening to a dance track, and the wording was 'I'm so glad you stayed, I'll be with you till the end". I was about to go down my usual thought process of "poor me, that didn't happen!", next track, move on quickly, when I suddenly thought I could change the lyrics' meaning around and make it all about me. I'm glad I stayed with me! I'll be with myself till the end!

I started to apply it to other songs, and it worked for almost all. Instead of skipping the love songs when they came on, I just mentally made them fit myself. It was so empowering. It made me realise that I could love myself. I could be there for myself and trust myself. For most of my life I had been relying on other people for that. Waiting for others to give me attention, tell me how beautiful I was, how clever I was. For my husband to tell me I was a wonderful mother, a great wife, that he would never leave me or hurt me. Well, all of that became utter bullshit, and now I had to do it for myself. And I realised that I could. I didn't actually need anyone else to validate and affirm me. That's what those songs taught me.

"I will always love you" "All of me"

"Thinking about you" "At last"

"I've got you under my skin"

I could go on, but you get the idea. Google 'love songs' and read or listen to the lyrics. You will see what I mean.

Music is meant to be emotive and sometimes, it is good to have a cry. I've done it a lot! But it must be balanced with realising that you will be ok. You are enough just as you are, without someone else to tell you they love you, you are beautiful, you are amazing, you are gorgeous, you are everything. Tell it to yourself!

You are the only one you can rely on 100%. The only one you can trust 100%. And the only one you really will be with until the end. Fact. Guarantee. This is not me being cynical or negative. I like the fact that I can rely on myself, that I know myself and I know my mind. That's the way it should be. We shouldn't put the responsibility on anyone else to have to do or be anything for us. It's not anyone else's responsibility to be a certain way to please us or to look after us. Once I realised this, I understood that maybe I had put quite a lot of pressure on my husband over the years to be a certain way, relying heavily on him for praise and validation and to tell me I was a good wife, a good mother and a good friend. Now, I know all that without having to look for others to reassure me.

I started making playlists of music that would remind me to keep fighting. Remind me of how strong I could be. To remind me of what being a single woman could mean. Not sadness and being lonely. Not abandonment and disappointment. But power and freedom, choices and adventure, pride and fulfilment.

Now, there's also another type of music I started using a few years ago, and that was music set to a specific frequency. Everything in the universe is based on vibration. That's why crystals and other energy healing tools work so well because they help balance our frequencies or vibrations, physically, mentally and emotionally. Music is no different. I will not explain the science of it all here because I'm not qualified to, but if you google music frequencies or Solfeggio frequencies you will find some fascinating information.

There are frequencies or vibrational sounds of music that resonate with our different chakras. For example, the frequency that resonates with the heart chakra is said to be 639hz. Listening to this can help with healing old traumas and wounds and opening ourselves up for love. I bought some ridiculously expensive wind chimes and hung them in the centre of my house, as instructed by the energy practitioner I bought them from, and the sound when I move them is wonderfully peaceful and relaxing. Sometimes, I carry them around the house and ring them as I go, and it almost feels like a fresh breeze has blown through. The house feels lighter, calmer and more peaceful.

When my marriage was falling apart, and I felt like my world was, too, I used these frequencies to help me sleep. By the time I went to bed, I was often so distraught over the helplessness of what I was feeling that sleep became impossible. I would lie awake for hours replaying conversations or things happening, trying to make sense of why I couldn't fix things. The solfeggio frequencies and healing music

I listened to weren't magic. I didn't immediately fall into a long and peaceful sleep, but like all the other tools I've spoken about in this book, they helped me to cope; they gave me an edge I needed.

At one time, I was feeling so anxious that when I tried to relax at night it was impossible. My body would twitch and jerk as if I was trying to escape myself. (It's probably a good thing that by then we had separate bedrooms!) When I listened to these sounds, they seemed to calm me after a while so I could drift off to sleep for a bit. I also knew that if I played them in my space, my bedroom, my office, wherever I could, that it would help calm any fractured energy.

The reason this chapter is called music and sound is that something else I found was wonderful, almost like a reset button was sound healing. For a few months, I went to a group meditation where we would all lie down on yoga mats, and the person leading the meditation would use singing bowls and a huge gong. I don't think I've ever experienced quite a transformation from how I felt going into the studio to leaving. It was like I'd walked in all muddy and dirty and walked out like I'd had a wonderfully refreshing shower, all clean and energised again. The guy doing it would walk around the room and gently hold the bowl over us, over our heads usually. At least, I think so, as I had my eyes closed. All I know is that when he rang it close to me, I could feel the vibration in every part of my body. It felt like all my energy cells were being shaken up and put back in their correct places. I felt so wonderfully balanced and harmonised after.

I use a lot of these things even now in my everyday life. I have the wind chimes still hanging in the centre of my home. I have another set that hangs in a back room that are tuned to the frequency of air because I'm a Gemini, which is an air sign. They emit the most amazingly gentle and soothing sounds.

Unless I need to concentrate on something, I always have music playing. I've used music as a tool to change my state and change my vibration for so long, that I can tell instantly if the song or piece isn't suited to me at that moment, so I change it. If I'm not having a great day, if I'm feeling sad or anxious I'll be extra careful about the music I listen to and will deliberately choose something upbeat. Maybe some dance music or some beautiful classical like Mozart or Bach.

It's been said that forgiveness is a gift you give

yourself, and I agree with that. There's a later chapter all about the benefits of that. But music is a gift we can easily give ourselves. We don't need a fancy sound system, although that's nice, all we need is our mobile phone and a little Bluetooth speaker or headphones. It's looking for opportunities, too. Taking the time to start something playing before we start driving, popping on some inspiring music in the morning or some soothing music at night, doing that instead of watching TV. I like to listen to music as I cook, drive, when I'm travelling, definitely when I'm cleaning, it makes it all go faster, oh and when I'm mowing the lawn.

Like anything else, it's a habit, a great one and so easy to incorporate into everyday life.

Something happens sometimes when listening to music, and that too can be a healing tool. It requires a certain amount of not caring what you look like, though! Sometimes, you can't seem to have one without the other, and that's the subject of my next chapter.

# CHAPTER SIX
# RHYTHMS OF RELEASE

---

*Dancing My Way to Freedom*


*"Dance is the hidden language of the soul."*

Martha Graham

Naturally, this follows on from the last chapter as sometimes, no matter how dreadful a dancer you are, you can't help yourself. I don't consider myself a good dancer (awful, actually), but I love to do it. I used to be self-conscious when I was younger and would only wobble about slightly unless I'd had a drink or two, but as I've gotten older, I don't care. It's a wonderful part of being in your fifties that I never expected. That you don't give a shit anymore about so many things. Things that used to worry me in my twenties and thirties don't anymore. I look back and can hardly believe I put so much store by what other people thought of me, my hair, how I dressed, how I sounded, what I talked about. It's ridiculous now I think about it.

So now, when I want to dance, I do. Very often, it's on my own in my living room, which is wonderful, as I can pretend I'm singing like Celine Dion and dancing like Beyoncé. I can assure you, however, that there is no resemblance to either when I catch myself in the mirror or hear my voice. But it does something to me. It seems to release any tension, any stress, any anxiety.

I found that I could get the high I used to need

a large whiskey to reach. Putting on some beautiful music I could get lost in or some dance music with a fantastic beat and literally dancing around my coffee table, into the hallway, around my dining table and back into the living room, out of breath but smiling and feeling great. It makes me feel alive, the blood is pumping, and my body is moving. Like music, dance raises my vibration. It's like an automatic injection of feel-good.

Dance used to be something I did when I went to parties or concerts. I never thought of it as a regular thing I could do and something that would help me on my healing journey. It's to do with music and movement. Our bodies are made to move. It's not natural we sit in front of a computer all day and then sit on a sofa all evening. We were designed to move and be active. It's a way of releasing stuck energy and emotions. Think back to our ancestors, not even far back. People moved so much more. Before cars and computers, trains and TV, there was so much more moving around. To get anywhere it was a bicycle or walking. Work was more active both in and out of the home. Because our lives are so sedentary now, we should be aware of moving and the easiest way to do that is to put on some music and, as Lady Gaga said, just dance!

Sometimes, I'd really get into it and letting my body go with the music and the beat and then suddenly, I'd start sobbing. Huge, deep howls of pain and despair. At first, it scared me, the strong emotions I was feeling, the suddenness of it, but then I realised how good I felt after. There was a calmness as if I'd gotten rid of another layer of pain and hurt. My body knew that it was in a safe space, that things needed to leave. I'd added another tool to the kit. Once I realised how good it was, I was even more aware of letting my body do its own thing, tuning in to my emotions, and if I needed to cry, I would. If I needed to enjoy the movement, I did.

I think, too, that the more I did it, the less inhibited I became. It's like my body was learning what it liked to do and how it liked to feel. Although it was just me in my living room, it was like shadowboxing. I had read about the concept of shadowboxing a few weeks earlier. It's a technique that famous boxers like Jim Corbett and Gene Tunney use and that Billy Graham used. It's a sort of pretending. So Jim Corbett would practice throwing a punch at an imaginary opponent in the mirror so when he met him in the ring, his body and mind already knew what to do. Billy Graham would preach his sermons to cypress stumps in a Florida swamp before going out to speak to live audiences.

What made me think my dancing in my living room was like shadowboxing is that I read about a woman who was nervous in social situations. She and her husband were often invited to parties and other social events, and when she got there, she would be so nervous she wouldn't be able to think of anything to say to anyone. It was suggested to her she practice at home. She set up her living room like a party room, with chairs and imagined various guests. She would go up to them and make conversation and interact with them with no fear or nervousness. She discovered that the next time she was at a social event with her husband, she was confident and relaxed and enjoyed it and chatted to the guests like she did in her make-believe party at home.

The next time I went out with my friends to a live music event in a nearby town in the summer, I felt freer than I ever had before to enjoy the music and dance. I didn't worry so much what people thought. My body was remembering what it felt like to be free and dance around my living room, the venue was a little different.

One thing I learned through this is that often, we tell ourselves that we can't do things because we are not very good. Or someone has commented about something we do, often years previously, and it's stuck. My parents danced. They were ballroom dancers, not professionally, just for fun, although they won quite a few competitions, so I grew up seeing them often dancing in the living room when I was a child. When I left home and started going to parties, someone commented on my lack of dance skills, and that was it, for years and years. It affected me, so I was self-conscious when I was in a situation where there was dancing, even though I loved to do it. It's taken me this long to enjoy it again. At the age I am now, though, and the way I feel, it wouldn't matter what anyone said, I'd still keep dancing!

Dancing takes energy though, a lot of it. My next chapter talks about something that has always interested me and that was to become my next healing tool. A tool that would not only give me the energy to dance but to get through my days. I needed not just physical but also mental and emotional energy.

# CHAPTER SEVEN
# FEEDING THE SOUL

---

*Nutrition's Role in Healing and
Strength*


*"Let food be thy medicine and medicine
be thy food."*

Hippocrates

I was raised by a mother who did not believe in buying cakes, biscuits or crisps and definitely no sodas. It was home cooking all the way and most things were made with brown flour and other healthy ingredients. This would have been fine if my mother enjoyed cooking, but sadly, gravy or custard covered most of my burnt dinners and deserts when I was younger. She was far too busy doing other things like making our clothes or doing crafts with us or taking me to the park to play or on a walk to pick flowers or berries. My sister and I often joke we  have exceptionally strong stomachs because of our childhood!

However, this led me on a path of always being interested in nutrition and alternative health. If we were sick, and I was often as a child with asthma, we were taken to an herbalist or homeopath before resorting to a regular doctor. I'm grateful that I learned about all this when I was young as it taught me that although my meals may not have been tasty, for the most part, they were healthy, and there was an alternative to getting things out of tins or the freezer or cooking in a microwave.

My own personal health journey started when I was pregnant with my first daughter. The thought that I was responsible for this little life inside, made me give up alcohol and caffeine as soon as I found out and be careful about what I ate. My mother-in-law had given me a book by Dr Vogel called The Nature Doctor and I followed to the letter all his suggestions about supplements and nutrition during my pregnancy. So much so that when my daughter was just four months old, and we went to a seminar to see Jan de Vries speak (he was a student of Dr Vogel) he used her as an example of what following a good nutritional program during pregnancy can result in. She was the picture of health. People used to stop me in the supermarket and tell me she was like the baby in the Gerber commercials!

That was it. This would be my life from then on. Two and a half years later, my second daughter was born, and I did the same. This was even more important this time around as I was hospitalised twice with pneumonia while I was pregnant with her. I made sure that what my daughters ate was healthy, but we balanced it out with treat visits to fast food places occasionally, too. We limited sugar, and Friday was sweetie day and they could choose a treat. Although, as my eldest daughter reminded me recently, it was usually chosen from a health food store.

I didn't set out to study health and nutrition; it sort of happened. When the girls would get sick, which was rare but inevitable, it would happen sometimes. I would research alternative ways of healing. This led me to learn about homeopathy, herbalism, aromatherapy, and so much more. It was such a good feeling to give them something that would have no side effects, but that would help them get well.

When my eldest was just nine months old we had moved to Wales to a rather cold house, and she developed a cough. I found a homeopathic remedy that stopped it dead. I was so happy and relieved as if I'd taken her to the doctor, she would probably have been prescribed antibiotics. I have to say that I am definitely not against conventional medicine. It has its place. However, for me, if there is a more natural alternative, I will always go for that first.

When I was rushed to hospital with pneumonia, I would have died if I hadn't had access to antibiotics. As would both my nephews, who had very serious health issues, one at birth and one at two years old. I'm grateful that I live in a place where I have a choice, and I'm grateful that I have the knowledge to make that choice.

So, back to nutrition, I digressed a little. I realised that the saying 'you are what you eat' is so true. I'm not talking about indulging in the occasional chocolate bar or fast-food burger. I mean what we eat day in and day out. Our habits. How we eat, when we eat and how much we eat. What we eat can also affect our mood too. It's everything, as it directly affects our body and our energy.

Sadly, we do not get enough nutrients from our food anymore. The soil is not as good quality as it once was, and even if we are buying organic there is no guarantee that the soil is perfect or that pesticides or contaminants don't drift onto them from the air. We do our best, but we often need extra vitamins and supplements.

When facing a challenge or experiencing trauma, it is even more important to be aware of our nutrition. We need all the help we can get! A poor diet will only lead to further issues and problems.

I've always been quite a foodie. I love food! My husband and I used to love planning our meals or where to go for dinner if we were eating out. However, when I found out about his betrayal, I couldn't eat. I lost my appetite. I would go all day and then realise that I had forgotten to eat. So, I started adding it to my daily list so I would have at least one meal a day. I also knew that as I was not eating as much as I should, and that what I ate had to be of good quality and very healthy. I started to up my vitamin supplements and add other things to my diet to keep up my strength.

For example, if I were having a salad, I would add some hemp seeds to it which are nutritionally dense and high in protein with a lot of vitamins and minerals. If I made soup or stew, I would add herbs like dandelion or burdock root, seaweed or some tulsi basil, which is calming. I always add garlic and ginger, too, if appropriate, to strengthen my immune system. I would also add some Ayurvedic supplements like ashwagandha or shatavari, which are both good for stress and anxiety. It's so easy to add things like this, and  it hardly changes the taste but makes a meal so much more valuable nutritionally.

Another thing I would do and still do is that if I didn't feel like eating, I would make myself a hot chocolate with cacao powder and add some medicinal mushroom powders like reishi or cordyceps for energy and to boost my immune system or lion's mane to help me focus. To sweeten it, I would add some maple syrup. If I'm feeling lazy, I will just mix the mushroom powders with some store-bought chocolate almond milk.

Juicing and smoothies are another way to get a densely packed nutritional boost. My go-to for juicing is carrot, cucumber, courgette, a lemon or two and ginger. I usually make enough for about three days, so I do not have to wash the juicer every day. For my smoothies, I will whizz up a banana with some blueberries, raspberries (fresh or frozen), any other fruit I have around, and half a cucumber or courgette, not forgetting to pop in a teaspoon or two of mushroom powder, and you have a perfect summer health boost. Also added to this would be a big teaspoon of moringa powder. This supplement is nutritious and high in antioxidants, vitamins and minerals.

Over the years, I did quite a good job of keeping my family healthy and now my daughters do it for themselves. If we are taught things as children, it is easier to incorporate them into our adult lives. I'm grateful that I could teach them this as my mother taught me. I expanded on it as I studied more and read more each year. Probably the most important way I passed on my knowledge was by example. My girls saw me eating healthy, being balanced and reaping the benefits.

Although it's important to think about nutrition and what we put into our bodies every day, it's even more important when we are under stress because our bodies need good fuel more than ever. For me, it was vital for me to keep up my health and energy when my world was falling apart. Because I was already in the habit of eating well, I didn't have to do much more than make an effort and force myself to eat well. Because I already knew what would give my immune system a boost and energise me and keep me from getting sick, I had to do it.

I didn't think of nutrition as a tool until I started writing notes for this book. I listed all the things that had got me through, and it seemed natural to add this. Another side benefit too is that it's fun and very satisfying to plan a nice meal for yourself. To buy the ingredients and take the time to cook a nutritious and healthy meal for you. It's another act of self-care, and it feels good to do it, not to please other people or to entertain, but just because you want to love yourself, nourish your body and because you deserve it.

# CHAPTER EIGHT
# CIRCLE OF STRENGTH

---

*The Unseen Bonds of Friendship*

*"Friendship is born at that moment
when one person says to another,
'What! You too? I thought I was the
only one.'"*

- C.S. Lewis

For so many years I had a good marriage. Much better than most others I saw. We were each other's best friends, and we did everything together. Over the years, I had a lot of friends. We lived all over the world, so I had friends in many countries. I won't say that I took them for granted, but I never felt like I needed them in my life as much as I needed my husband. They were an add-on.

I was fortunate enough to have very close friendships, mostly when my girls were little. Mothers bonding, that sort of thing. We needed each other for support and for a chance to hang out with adults as we were all stay-at-home mums. I didn't consciously think to myself that I needed them, but I was so very grateful for them.

However, as my daughters grew up and had their own lives, my husband and I started to travel more and spend more time with just each other. We ran a business together, too, so it was a 24/7 relationship, and for many years it worked wonderfully. Until it didn't! In the years between my girls being little and growing up, my friendships had gone from hanging out with other mums to doing things as couples because the girls were now old enough not to need babysitters. We could go for meals and drinks and movies with other couples. This was lovely, but I don't think I formed any close friendships. It was more about having fun and hanging out.

When my world fell apart, and I realised that my marriage was over, one of the first thoughts that came once I could actually think again was that I needed my friends like never before, or I would not survive this. I realised how many friends I had. Friends I had kept in touch with sporadically over the years because we didn't live in the same country anymore and friends I had local to me and everything between. I am the sort of person who is not very good at asking for help. It's usually a last resort. If I'm feeling like it's the worst day of my life and someone asks me how I am, I'll say, great, I'm fine, yeah, thanks. But there was a voice inside of me that said, swallow your pride and reach out, you need this like never before. So, I did. I messaged all my friends in the USA, Egypt, Thailand, France, England and Wales. Once my friends here in France heard, they became my support system. From visits to my home for a cup of tea and a hug to inviting me to their homes and to taking me out for drinks and lunches and just basically welcoming me with open arms into their circle that I had only been on the periphery of for years because I wasn't always here.

It made me realise how much we need each other and to be there for each other. That was brought home very much this last year. My lovely friend Sam, who I spoke about in the yoga chapter, was one of my biggest strengths, along with her partner. Then, her beautiful and kind mother, who also had welcomed me and comforted me with loving arms and a wise heart, became sick, very sick. It was my turn to give back. It's so true what's been said about helping others takes you out of your own problems. I watched my friend nurse her mother through six horrible months, right to the end, and I was privileged to be a support. Now it was my turn to hold her and let her cry. This is how deep and meaningful friendships are made. It's not necessarily the fun times, the parties or the socialising, but being there for each other when you are at your lowest and knowing there is someone's house and arms you can run to when it all gets too much.

My friends who could not hug me in person sent me messages of love and a 'Hey how are you doing', 'I'm here for you' and 'I'm thinking of you'.

One friend offered to hop on a plane from where she lived in Colorado if I needed her. Knowing she absolutely would have done it if I'd asked her to was all I needed. Plus, being there on the end of the phone and hearing me sob and just listening, not offering advice, just listening and being there for me. It all added up to remind me I was loved. I needed that reminder, too. I'd never needed my friends like that before. We need friends when we are young and throughout our lives, but as an adult, I'd got to my 50s before realising the priceless value of having friends that love you for exactly who you are, unconditionally. I don't think I'd ever had that before. The friends I had up to then had mostly been part of the same religion I was in, a high-control religion where friendships outside of the faith are highly discouraged, and most friendships in the faith are conditional on you continuing on that same path, staying in that same club.

So, I learned an important lesson and one I will never forget. We need other people. If you are like me and often isolate yourself and try and fix everything on your own, when times are challenging, when you are at a low point, take my advice and reach out. It's humbling to realise that we can't do it all by ourselves, and it does make life richer.

Another benefit for me is that it has made me even more aware of being there for other people as they were for me. I don't just mean the ones that helped me. I mean everybody. How long does it take to send a quick text to a sick friend to say we hope they feel better soon. It takes seconds to write a message to that person we know who is going through a hard time and believe me, it can often change that person's day from being an endurance test where your only goal is to make it to bedtime to a reminder that there are people that love you and care about you, which brightens a day considerably.

I would make this chapter about girlfriends, how much we women need other women in our lives, but I have a few very special friends who are men and that were my support system, too, so it seemed very unfair. Three come to mind that were so wonderful when I was so low. Different messages than my women friends, and one took it upon himself to do his best to make me smile when it was the last thing I wanted to do, with funny jokes and silly memes. What I've realised is that we need a whole arsenal of friends. We need the one who makes us laugh, we need the one we can cry with, we need the one who will feed us when we are too weak to feed ourselves and we need to be that friend to others. It's so easy to get caught up in day-to-day life and think someone else in the group of friends will help so and so, but we can't expect people to be there for us unless we are there for them.

It takes bravery to be a good friend. You have to open your heart and risk being laughed at when you share ideas or forgotten about when they are busy with things that are actually more important than you! But being brave enough to be a friend and have a friend is one of the ways I got through the hardest year of my life.

# CHAPTER NINE
# SMALL WINS, BIG CELEBRATIONS

*Embracing Every Step of Progress*

*"Treat every small victory like you just
won the Superbowl."*

Lewis Howes

I learned this from my mother when I was a child. Being brought up in a religion that didn't allow much celebrating, no birthdays or holidays, meant that celebrating something was a big deal. So, my mother used to look for little things to celebrate. When we were out doing our preaching work, if we met someone nice and they listened or took our magazines, she would take me for a coffee and a cake, or we'd buy a chocolate bar. It is a practice that I carried on throughout my life, often just in my head, but it's a practice I've done more of lately.

When you are on a healing journey, it's important to see progress. So often, it can seem as if we are making progress, and then the next day or hour or minute, we feel like we are back where we started. So, celebrating wins means we have concrete proof we are progressing.

There's no timeline or speed counter, either. Everyone's journey is different, and some parts of our journey may take longer than we anticipated, too. We can be impatient to get to the other side, to be healed, but that is something that can't be rushed. It has its own pace. Plus, it's a journey, not a destination. But the moment we notice we are somewhere we wanted to be, that we have reached a new level, we need to stop and acknowledge it. The level can be a huge leap, or it can be a small step, either way, it's progress. The celebrating doesn't even need to be anything more than patting ourselves on the back, and thanking ourselves for caring enough to do this. But we must stop and take in that we are a little or a lot further on our journey.

I've had so many wins this past year and in the years since I started my healing journey. It seems like a simple thing, but for me, a huge win was waking up in the morning happy and looking forward to the day instead of dreading it. Wins can be learning to set boundaries and then noticing yourself implementing them. It can be putting yourself first and learning to say no.

A lot of my wins were milestones. When you go through a breakup or a loss, for the first year, there are so many firsts. Apart from obvious dates like anniversaries, birthdays and holidays, there are also a lot of other firsts. The first time you go for a walk on the route you both used to take. The first time you do anything by yourself that you both used to do together. These are big things, don't minimise them.

One of my happy places is the forest at the

back of my house. It used to be a place we would walk together. The first time I went by myself, I didn't see many trees. It's a miracle I didn't fall into the river as I was crying so much, desperately hoping I wouldn't bump into any locals who already think me strange being an English woman in a little French village and now walking through the forest sobbing. But that was the only time I was like that, the first time. Oh, I've cried in that forest so many times, but that was the only time I did it because it was a first; the next time was still sad but not as bad. And slowly, it became my sanctuary, my happy place, the place I could go to feel refreshed and energised if I was having a bad day.

I celebrate my wins when it strikes me as a win. So, when I notice that I've accomplished something, I congratulate myself. Sometimes, it's a YES! And I look in the mirror and tell myself I'm awesome. Sometimes, it's a cake from the patisserie, and sometimes, it's curling up on the sofa with a bag of crisps, a whiskey and my latest book because I'm particularly proud of how far I've come.

Some wins are big, and some are small. Some of my big wins were surviving our wedding anniversary, doing the five-hour drive up to my sisters for the first time, taking the car to the garage and it passing it's *controle technique* (MOT), finding an artisan to fit new windows for my house before winter and paying for it all myself, and hitting that one year mark as a completely different person than I was. Someone who I liked and admired, someone I was proud of and someone rebuilding their life and loving it. Someone who could now contemplate the future without fear.

Some of my small wins were filling the car up with fuel and realising that I was doing it all myself and learning how to check tyre pressure and oil levels, hosting friends for the first time on my own, getting a huge wood delivery for winter and stacking it all myself and being ok with locking up the house at night and going up to bed on my own.

I made a vow to myself in the days after I found out about my husband's betrayal that I would come through this with dignity, bravery and courage. I was so determined that I wrote those words on three post it notes and stuck them on my fridge. I also had a mug made with the same words so I could remember it each day as I drank my tea. I wanted to look back and not regret my actions.

Of course, I wanted to rip his head off and

chop off other bodily parts, and it was a long time before I was in a place where I wasn't happy when I heard about his misfortunes since I left. However, I promised myself that I would act with dignity, so I kept all those thoughts to myself and the pillows I screamed into, and sometimes venting to my sister. I was determined to keep my dignity.

The bravery and courage came in to help me rebuild my life when I had no idea what that life would look like. To imagine a life on my own was impossible, so I followed my sister's advice and took it one hour at a time until I got to a place where I thought more than a day ahead at a time.

When I hit the year mark, I realised that was a huge win. That I could look back and see that those words that were my mantra became how I was. I had kept my dignity, and I was brave and had courage.

Acknowledging this was me celebrating, being ok with telling myself I was a winner, I was proud of myself and who I had become.

Which probably leads me to my biggest win, and that was being happy to be single. I realised one day, I was blissfully happy, content and at peace. There was no man in my life, and I wasn't talking to anyone or going on dates. I wanted this time for me. For the first time in my life, I felt like this. At fifty-four! I didn't miss anything, I didn't need anything. I was self-sufficient, and it felt so good to feel this level of contentment. Once I felt that, it was as if my healing took a huge jump. I started to let go of things on a whole new level. Not just events of the past year but the hurt of my mother and brother's rejections, my childhood abuse, losing my community when I left the religion. It all drifted away even further.

And then I started to celebrate each day because each day was feeling like a party. I was waking up happy, I was living my purpose, I had a beautiful life with my family and my friends in a beautiful place and most important, I was at peace. That deep inner peace and contentment I had finally reached was worth celebrating.

That I had learned to love myself was worth celebrating. That I had learned to set boundaries, that I had taken the time to get to know myself, to learn what I want and don't want, to learn what my biggest goals and dreams are. These were definitely worth celebrating.

Celebrating our wins is a way of being grateful, too. We are showing gratitude for ourselves and the work we've done to get to where we are. We are being grateful for the precious life we have, even if it looks different from the one we originally envisioned. I read a quote a long time ago, and it said that god's gift to us is our lives. Our gift to god is what we do with it. And celebrating our wins is celebrating the wonder of our lives, and the more we celebrate, the more we win, and the more we win, the more we celebrate. It never stops!

# CHAPTER TEN
# FROM PEN TO FLAMES

---

*Writing and Burning for Emotional Liberation*

*"Writing is an act of burning, a ritual of renewal."*

\- Unknown

Writing. Reading. Burning. Three small things, when all put together are powerful. My reiki teacher taught me this years ago, and although at first it seemed dramatic, it works. It's simple. You take a notebook or a few sheets of paper, not a fancy notebook because you will destroy what you write.

First, think of a situation that is upsetting you, something you just can't let go of or get past. Maybe it's something relatively minor like your sister was short with you or forgot your birthday, or maybe it's something major, like the pain you are feeling from a betrayal or an abandonment or loss. It doesn't matter; whatever it is, start writing about it. Don't think about what you are writing, just write. Let all the emotions pour out: the pain, the despair, the anger, the disappointment, and whatever else comes up. What you will find as you write is that emotions come up that you were not expecting. To get the most value from this exercise you need to just let the words flow without judgement. I guarantee you will be surprised at how much comes up and how deep you can allow yourself to go.

One of the first times I did it was trying to process the hurt I felt from my mother cutting off contact with me after I left the faith I was a part of for most of my life. That I'd left because of the same reason (child abuse) that had put my father in prison years earlier, which my mother knew about, had left me feeling this pain and bewilderment. Being a mother myself, I couldn't fathom how she could not want to talk to me. I could imagine nothing either of my daughters could do that would make me want to not be in their lives.

It's amazing how the universe knows just what you need when you need it. One day, my husband and daughter were going out to a local *vide grenier* (flea market) and asked if I wanted to go with them. I said no, but as soon as they left, I had this overwhelming feeling I wanted to go after all and that I was missing out by not going. I didn't want to call them and ask them to come back for me, so I thought I'd leave it up to the universe. I asked that if it were right for me, they would come back. As the minutes ticked by and they didn't come back, I started to get upset wondering why the universe wasn't working things out for me. Then, out of nowhere I remembered about the burn and release I'd been told about.

I knew they'd be out for a few hours, so I took the opportunity. I started to write, and as I started to write, I cried. (At the end of this chapter are prompts you can use, like the ones I used.) I wrote about how abandoned I felt, asking how she could choose to listen to man-made rules in her organisation over her daughter. I wrote about how hurt I was that she hadn't protected me when I was a child. And then, out of nowhere, this huge howl erupted from me, and I started sobbing and screaming and releasing a pain so deep I didn't even know pain could go that low. It was like it came from the utter depths of my soul. If you can imagine crying so hard you can't even breathe, you'll know what I mean. I cried the hardest I had ever cried.

It went on for a while, and in between, I was writing. I was shocking myself with what I was writing; I didn't realise how angry I was. I wrote terrible things, things I didn't know I could think, let alone write. And then, like turning off a tap that had been gushing full speed, it stopped, and I felt a level of relief and peace I'd never felt before in my life. Like a huge weight I'd been carrying on my own for years had been lifted off my back. I sat on the floor in my hallway and just was. I didn't think, I just sat rather stunned, and I let myself enjoy the feeling. It felt like something big had happened.

The second part is after you've taken a break and processed what has come up with the writing, you read it out loud. After doing that, you burn it. You can use visualisation here, too, especially as you watch it burning. You can imagine that all the anger, hurt and pain that you've released is floating away from you and that it is being transmuted from negative to positive. Whatever works for you, this is just an extra, unnecessary for the process.

I have a fire basket outside, so as it was summer, I thought it was a good way to burn my pages safely. I took them outside, along with a few remaining things that my mother had given me. I felt as if I had to symbolically get rid of all the reminders. I stood by that fire with my voice cracking and tears running down my face, reading what I had written and, for the first time, seeing the depth of my pain. I ripped the paper into smaller bits and fed them to the flames. I watched it all burn down to ashes. The paper that had my pain, a scarf she had given me and a pair of earrings.

As I stood there, I realised why I wasn't meant to go to the *vide grenier* that morning. Why events had conspired to give me the house to myself, something that rarely happened. I would never have cried and howled and screamed like I did if my family had been there. I may have done the burn and release, but it would not have been on this deep level, maybe just some quiet tears. I felt as if I'd been gifted this space and time to add another layer to my healing.

It taught me a lesson, though, not to keep emotions in that need to come out. In the following years, if I needed to release, cry, vent or shout, I would go for a drive in my car. When driving you are alone and safe to make whatever sounds you need to. I must mention two things, though. One is to be careful of doing it in busier traffic; you get funny looks! And the other point is more serious. Sometimes, it's safer to pull over to the side of the road to let go. The emotions that come up can be powerful and distracting.

In the year following the breakup of my marriage, I used this method a few times. Once, I went to the river and burned what I'd written and watched the ashes float away. That seemed very symbolic. Another occasion that stands out was towards the end of the year after we'd been separated for just over fourteen months. I was in a place where I wanted to start forgiving, but I knew I needed to write it out. I was finally ready to do so; I could feel it.

I wrote pages and pages, pouring out all my sadness and pain, how much I missed him and our beautiful life, and then releasing him, telling him I was ready to forgive and let him go.

The night I did this was the full moon, and just over a week later was New Year's Eve, and as this was almost the end of the worst year of my life, I decided that I would read it out loud every night until New Year's Eve and then I would burn it. As I read it each night, I got closer and closer to a place of forgiveness, or rather a start on the road to forgiveness. At first, I cried all the way through, but as the week progressed, an amazing thing happened. I started finally to think of happy memories and times we'd had together. To remember how much love we had between us and how grateful I was to have had that in my life for so long.

I had a goal of sending him a text on NYE and wishing him well. This seemed like it would be a milestone for me. I knew, though, that it had to be genuine. We weren't in regular communication, but I wanted to be at peace. To send the message, I wanted to feel in my heart that I meant it and that I did wish him peace and happiness for the next year. When I first wrote those pages, I didn't know if I would be at a place on NYE where I could honestly wish him well. As the week progressed, though, I started to feel differently. It was as if it was all being released, and all that was left were memories of the pain but actually feeling it, had seemed to drift away. When the last day of the year came, I knew in my heart that I would be able to send him that text, and that was such a huge moment. The realisation that I could forgive him and let go, to move on with my life. I wanted to start the new year not as a survivor but as someone who was living again and creating a life. I wanted to start again in a big way. Unlike the previous new year, when I was so frightened of the coming year and what it would bring, this year I was excited for it to start, for my plans and the things I wanted to do. As I burned those pages on the last night of that sad and pain-filled year, I was saying goodbye to the life I had lived and known and the dreams we had together. But now I had new dreams, and they were my own, and that felt so good.

Here are writing prompts and questions that can help you get started on this:

1. What specific actions or behaviours have hurt me the most?

2. How has this hurt affected my

emotions, thoughts, and daily life?
3.  I'm angry that...
4.  I hate that you...
5.  I'm hurt that...
6.  I feel disappointed because...
7.  I am afraid that...
8.  It makes me sad that...
9.  I am scared because...
10. I hate feeling....

Use the above prompts to get you started on your writing. Remember it's for you. Don't think about spelling, grammar or what you say. Just write and let it all out.

# CHAPTER ELEVEN
# RELEASE TO HEAL

---

*The Essential Power of Crying,*
*Screaming, and Shouting*

*"But a mermaid has no tears, and*
*therefore she suffers so much more."*

Hans Christian Andersen

I was driving home one chilly but sunny Sunday afternoon from a beautiful village about 30 minutes away. It was my first time going out for a drink by myself since my breakup, and I had been to a local brewery where they have live music on a Sunday afternoon. I sat there feeling so strange on my own amidst groups and couples. I toughed it out, trying to look like I was relaxed and enjoying it, but just holding it together and feeling like everyone was staring at me, the only single person there, like I had a huge flashing neon sign on my head. The singer had a beautiful voice, but when she started to sing La Vie en Rose, it was too much. I went up and paid for my drink before running outside and bursting into tears. That had been one of our favourite songs. I walked down the street sobbing and not caring what the people I passed thought, got in the car and started to drive home. I couldn't stop crying, and suddenly, it turned to absolute anger and rage, and I started shouting and screaming out all my hurt and pain. I was saying things I couldn't say in person but that my heart needed to get rid of. I knew it wasn't safe to be driving, so I quickly pulled over and sat and shouted at the top of my lungs, screaming louder than I thought possible with a voice I didn't even recognise as my own. The sounds were raw and primitive and from a place I didn't know existed. It seemed to go on for a long time but was probably only a few minutes. When it stopped, I was drained, and my throat hurt.

I drove home and sat curled up on the sofa with not an ounce of energy left even to make a cup of tea. I pulled a blanket over me and laid my head on the oversized cushion. I thought about what had happened and how, if we let it, the body knows exactly what we need. When it needs to release emotions, it's so important for us to give ourselves the space to allow that to happen. I don't like to imagine what would be happening to my body if I had not allowed that to come out. I know it's right to allow this because the way I feel after is calm and peaceful and like a weight has been lifted.

We can all find a space to do this when we need to. Even if it's locking yourself in the bathroom and shouting and screaming into a pillow or inventing a trip to the supermarket so you can be alone in the car. The body needs to release emotions, and we now know that not doing this and dealing with how we are feeling causes illness and disease, or more correctly, dis-ease.

I woke up one day with terrible lower back pain. I'm not someone who has ever suffered from a bad back, so this was not normal. I'd had a few bad days, sad days where I was just crying a lot and wondering how I would make a life for myself. I sat on the sofa in a lot of pain and decided to look through some old photos. On our last wedding anniversary, the girls had made a beautiful gift for us of photos through the years of the four of us on our travels, enjoying life, being a family, all carefully pasted into a pale green leather-bound album that they'd had custom made. It was meant to be something to be treasured, and they had both worked hard on planning it all. Looking back now I can see that it was a precious gift and that on the last wedding anniversary we had together, we were celebrating as a family, the four of us. Almost like it had come full circle and was a fitting end. Although I didn't appreciate that until much later.

It just hit me we were no more. The beautiful family I had treasured and created was gone. I lay on the floor and cried, and the grief was so deep and painful, I could hardly breathe. I curled up into a ball and just lay there on my side crying so hard for all that I had lost, all that had vanished from my life. After a while, I got myself together and sat back on the sofa. I took a few minutes to realise that my back pain was gone. Not just better but virtually gone. There was a twinge but nothing major. A few minutes earlier, I had been thinking there was something wrong, the pain was so bad, and that maybe I should go to the doctor.

That was another reminder of how powerful our emotions are, the mind-body connection. I had basically cured my pain by crying. I had always had such a tight rein on my emotions. Growing up in an abusive household where I had to hide what was happening to me and where I was constantly reminded that how I acted and looked was a direct reflection on not only our family but on God and the religion we were a part of meant that I often hid how I was feeling. Emotions and honest talk were definitely not encouraged. So obviously, when I became an adult, I saw no reason to change. I was always that person who was 'fine' or 'great thanks' even when I wasn't. I didn't let myself cry in movies because it felt silly, and it made my husband feel awkward.

However, once I started on my healing

journey, I found out how important it was to feel the feelings to acknowledge my emotions. I started allowing myself to feel more. The big breakthrough came when I went on a ten-day meditation course to develop psychic awareness. The course included twenty five meditations over the ten days. I had no idea what I was in for. By day two, I told the lady running the course that I doubted that I would make it to day ten. In the meditations, we explored our fears, our limiting beliefs, our hurt, our pain and our anger. I had never had to look so closely at myself before. I'd never had to think about how and why I felt the way I did about certain things, to confront the pain of my childhood, and my family relationships, my relationships with my daughters and the way I felt like I'd failed them in some ways, and my relationship with my husband which by then was on very wobbly ground.

In those ten days, I learned how to cry. I learned how to sit with my emotions, and feel them and release them. It was a life-changing ten days. On the day after I'd finished it, my sister messaged to say our father had died. I didn't even know he was sick, and I had not had contact with him since I was twenty-nine over twenty years previously. Now, that was a crazy set of emotions to deal with, and for the first time, I was on my own, not just physically because I was in Bangkok and my husband was in Phuket, but I no longer had his support. Even though we were still married and living together, he had become distant and uncaring , but before I'd had all the attention I could ever want from him.

So I cried in a confused way, not sure if I was sad because he'd died or sad because I wanted to be crying over a father who had died that I loved. I wanted to miss him; I wanted to feel that devastating loss, but I didn't. I just felt confused. But now I cried. I had never thought before that crying was a gift but now, I do.

So, most times when I feel like crying, I do. There are times when I have to hold it in, but I let myself feel however I feel. My sister once said that she couldn't believe how well I was coping with everything after my marriage breakup, but I feel that it was because I was living alone and was able to do all the things I needed to let myself heal, one of the most important being that I could cry whenever I needed to.

# CHAPTER TWELVE
# PATHWAYS TO PEACE

---

*Embracing Forgiveness for Personal
Freedom*

*"The weak can never forgive.
Forgiveness is the attribute of the
strong."*

Mahatma Gandhi

Phew this is a big one, and probably one of the hardest. As children we are taught about forgiveness, especially if we have siblings! Once we go to school it's inevitable someone will upset us, and we are given the forgiveness lecture by our parents or teachers. But we are never taught why we should forgive, at least, I wasn't. I was told it was something I should do. Forgive and forget, or forgive, but don't forget. Either way, it's all missing the point.

We don't forgive because we are being kind to the other person, or we are finally ok with what happened and can rise above it all. The reason we forgive is so we are not stuck in that situation anymore. It's so we can leave it where it belongs in the past. We don't want to have it in our present or carry it with us into the future. We forgive for ourselves, no one else. We forgive because we love ourselves enough to want to live with peace and not with anger or resentment. It doesn't matter if it's a small thing or a big thing. It's the same process, one just happens faster and is easier. It's a lot easier to forgive someone who cut you off in traffic than it is to forgive a parent for abandoning you or a partner for betraying you.

It's a process with no definite timeline. We are all different, and all our situations are different too. Not only that, but each time we come up against a situation that requires forgiveness, that is unique, too. There are no rules for this. Some people like to say there are, but I don't think so. It's such a personal thing to go through, and there are so many variables. One such challenge is that it is often much easier to forgive when something has been done to you, as opposed to when something affects a loved one. The hardest is when someone hurts your child, either physically or emotionally.

I remember when my daughter had her first serious boyfriend, and he broke up with her in a less than honourable way, over the phone while she was visiting us in France. To see her pain and sadness made me want to hop over to the UK and do dreadful things to him. I took a while to forgive the pain he had caused her. I would think I'd forgiven and then my mind would wander into the realms of possible ways to ruin his business or let his friends know how awful he was.

I learned the power of forgiveness many years ago. I had been reading a Jack Canfield book called The Success Principles. In it there's a chapter on forgiveness and a step-by-step process on how to do it. I followed it to the letter, as I felt it was time for me to forgive my father for his abuse of me when I was a child. I took a while to work through it and the night I finished it, I slept the deepest sleep of my life and felt like a weight had been lifted. That was only the start of it, however. It's not final; it's an ongoing process. You seem to go so far and then stop. I had started it, but it was still quite a while after that I could say I forgave him, and it was not affecting my life anymore.

As I'm writing this, I am trying to think how I would know when I have truly forgiven, and it's when I can think of that person in a neutral way. That thinking of them doesn't affect me, and I can remember happy memories and the good times we had together. I read once that forgiving means we don't let that person have control over us anymore. That is one of the main factors in why I work towards forgiveness. If someone has wronged me, why would I let them have space in my head and control my life. Holding on to anger, bitterness and resentment keeps me stuck in the past with them, and if you part ways and they are no longer part of your day-to-day life, you deserve to move on. You can't move on and let go if every time you think of them, you are planning their downfall or hoping that their life is a miserable mess.

In the previous chapter, I spoke about the burn and release protocol I was taught. This has helped me hugely on my forgiveness journey. I can't forgive if I keep it all bottled up inside me. It must go to get out of my head, my heart, my mind and my feelings. By writing it out, I can see it more objectively. I can say things I maybe can't or wouldn't say in person. I can give free rein to my emotions and my feelings. I can be as angry and upset as I want to on paper, and it feels good. We can't even think about forgiveness until we have acknowledged how much it hurts, how much pain we feel, and how disappointed we are by the other person's actions.

In the year after my marriage broke up, I wrote so many letters to my husband that I never sent. I told him exactly how I was feeling, I poured it all out. Every time after writing one, I would feel a little lighter, a little less like my head would explode until I didn't need to write them anymore. I didn't exactly forgive straight away or all at once. It seemed to come in stages and was a different process than when I forgave my father. I'm not sure why, maybe because what happened with my father was when I was a child, and I was already distanced from him and had a beautiful life I was living. This time, it was the end of spending 34 years with someone, and my heart wasn't just broken. It was smashed to pieces.

I knew it was important to my health in every way, though, mentally, emotionally and even physically. It took quite a few months before I could even contemplate forgiving, probably over a year. Once the thought was there, though, I explored it and decided it was time to start the process. I call it a process because when it's something that has affected your life in a big way, you can't just wake up one day and think, ok, that person is forgiven. It takes active work.

The first thing I started to do was spend part of my meditation each day working on it. At first, I would just try and see what it would feel like to forgive. Then, I used a visualisation that I had been taught. You imagine yourself on a beach with a stick in your hand, and you write the name of the person in the sand. When I tried to do this at first, I wasn't able to, I couldn't see it, I wasn't ready. So, I started to send him love, peace and good thoughts. After a while of doing this, I wrote his name in the sand. I cried the first few times I did it. Forgiveness is a form of letting go. You are breaking the control they have over you by what they did.

Another thing I did was what I spoke about in the previous chapter, on a full moon, which is a good time for things to conclude, I wrote a final letter. In it I told him I was letting him go and that I forgave him. I thanked him for the years we had together and how grateful I was that I knew what it was to love and be loved. I cried so hard writing it and then reading it out loud after over the next few days. The burning of it on New Year's Eve signified an ending and gave me a symbolic new start for the next year. I think sometimes we need cut-off points. A definite act that marks one part of our life as the past and the next part as the future.

It's not something that's finished. It will take much longer for me to forgive fully and completely, but I am well on my way, and I feel better for it. I know people who are bitter and angry because of past hurts, and I never want to be like that. Not only does it make your life miserable, but it causes health problems, too. I've seen that firsthand in my own family.

I'm so grateful that I learned the importance

of forgiving. I look at it as part of my self-care and self-love routine. It's not optional if I want to live a happy and full life. It's difficult, and some days you may feel as if you have gone backwards instead of forwards, but the most important thing to do is not to give up and think it's impossible to do. If you want to do it and will put in the time and effort, I can promise it brings peace and calm that is worth way more than the effort you put in because to feel like that is priceless.

# CHAPTER THIRTEEN
# NATURE'S EMBRACE

---

*Healing and Transformation Through*
*the Seasons of Life*

*"To find the universal elements enough;*
*to find the air and the water*
*exhilarating; to be refreshed by a*
*morning walk or an evening saunter...*
*to be thrilled by the stars at night; to be*
*elated over a bird's nest or a wildflower*
*in spring - these are some of the rewards*
*of the simple life."*

John Burroughs

I live in a small village that borders a beautiful forest. I can walk out of my front door, and in less than two minutes, I am walking in nature. I've always loved this, but I took a while to realise how essential this was to my healing and my mental health.

Nature gives, but it never takes, and it has so many lessons to teach us. The truth of this hit me one day as I was standing by the river and watching the leaves falling in autumn and being consumed and swept away. It has lessons on letting go and lessons on reliability, on community and on being authentic. Whatever lessons you can think of, whatever teachings there are, they are in nature.

As I walk into the forest, I am entering another world. There's a narrow path with a small canopy of trees that meet to form a beautiful green tunnel. Every time I go in, I feel like I am being welcomed with open arms. Like the forest is saying come on in, we've got you, you're not alone. Even though most of the time when I'm walking in the forest I am actually alone, I never feel as if I am. I feel safe and protected and no matter how awful I feel when I start my walk, I always feel so much better after. It feels like an energetic Xanax. I have walked in, barely able to breathe, with sadness that feels so heavy I can barely move one foot in front of the other, and I stand by the river or sit by my favourite tree, and I feel a calm and peace wash over me. An energy is shared with me so I always walk out feeling like I can carry on for longer.

I've told that tree things I've told no one else. I've begged for help and strength in a way that I never would with a human. Every time I feel it. I feel an energy and a sense that I don't have to do this alone. They are always there for me. I can always count on them. They always want me and welcome me. They never judge me or tell me what to do. They are just there to support. All I need to do to feel this is stop and be still. To stop thinking I am silly to imagine all this and just to believe. Because what fun is life if we don't use our imagination and allow ourselves to believe in the impossible and the illogical.

I've also been a big fan for years of earthing or grounding. In the summer, or not just summer, whenever it's warm enough, I go barefoot. Sometimes, on my bad days, even when it was frosty on the grass, I'd take my shoes off and stand there for a few minutes. The calm it gave me, the balancing I could feel in my body was well worth the chilly toes.

If I'm feeling stressed, walking in the garden barefoot or just standing for a while just takes it all out of me, as if it's draining down into the earth.

I'm one of those old-fashioned people who like to hang my washing on the line and only use the tumble dryer whenever necessary. My washing line is at the bottom of my garden, so it's another good opportunity to go barefoot, much to my old Portuguese neighbour's horror, who is constantly lecturing me on the awful things that could happen. Just a note, nothing ever has. Like anything else it's a habit, so whenever I can, I take my shoes off, in the garden, at the beach. Anywhere I can ground myself and be connected to the earth, I will.

Another way I have used nature in my healing is to have lots of plants around me in my home, especially where I work, in my office and on my desk. Apart from the fact that they look nice, taking care of them makes me stop and appreciate how wonderful they are. I see their growth and how they change and sometimes die, and I'm reminded of the lessons once again. I also took Miley's advice and I regularly buy myself flowers. Making my space beautiful and welcoming to be in, makes a difference to how I feel. There's a reason we buy flowers or a plant for someone who is sick or needs cheering up. It's about the beauty of nature, the energy and the reminders that we are all connected and we are never alone.

Watching the leaves fall off the trees is a powerful metaphor for letting go and healing. The leaves have to say goodbye to the safety of the tree and fall to the ground, knowing that they will become something else. The tree then stands there throughout the winter, not looking so pretty and often looking like it's dead. But it's what is going on inside that matters. Inside, it's resting, taking time to just be, and patiently waiting until spring, when it needs all its energy to blossom and grow new leaves. It reminds me that sometimes we need to do that, too. It's ok just to be, to rest, and to look like we are not doing anything or accomplishing anything. Sometimes I feel as if I have to show everyone that I'm busy and surviving and succeeding at rebuilding my life. But I don't. We don't always need to be doing, striving, building. Sometimes, we need to disintegrate like the caterpillar does before it becomes a butterfly. If the caterpillar didn't become a chrysalis and allow complete disintegration, it would never emerge on the other side, transformed into a beautiful butterfly.

When we allow ourselves that time to let go of the old part of ourselves and our former life, we allow transformation and with that transformation comes different thinking, new perspectives, and a whole new world. Anything that devastates us changes us. We can use that experience to our benefit for personal growth, and it's only by stopping and just giving ourselves time to be that we can see the possibilities. If we just keep on the treadmill of trying to survive, that's all we will ever do. We will never stop surviving, and we will forget how to live. The point of rebuilding my life was to get to a point of living again. My end goal was not surviving.

And sometimes nature reminds us that things die, and that's ok. We can't hold onto things forever. This summer my beautiful palm tree at the front of my house died. Apparently, it was a moth that laid eggs in the trunk, and it had affected a lot of other palms in my area. I tried everything to fix it, but eventually, I had to cut it down and have it taken away. That tree had been there since we bought the house, so it was hard to see it go.

I tried everything to fix my marriage, but that too was dead, and I had to accept that. Like the palm,

I remembered how beautiful it was at one time, the joy it gave me and how happy I was. Life is full of changes and we cannot control other people and make them the way we want them to be. What we can do, though, is allow the changes and work to a place where we are accepting of them. Now, I choose to remember the good times, not the bad. I've spent a lot of time thinking about the bad times, and that was necessary. I had to process it all and get to a place where I was ready to remember the good times. It doesn't just happen. Now, I don't remember my palm tree as it was before it was cut down. Ugly dead palm fronds and a bare trunk. I remember it when it shaded my kitchen window and was beautifully green and how happy it made me when I would come home and pull up outside in my car and I'd see it. That's how I remember it, and that's how I choose to remember my marriage. The years when we were a fabulous team, taking on the world, all the travelling we did together and how he would bring me a cup of tea every morning without fail exactly the way I liked it, how he never let me worry about anything to do with the car or the house, he took care of it all, and how proud he always was of me when I achieved anything. How often he told me he loved me and that

I was beautiful. How angry he would get if anyone ever upset me. Most of all how he was my best friend for most of my life. So yes, it's gone, but I had it. I have known what it is to love with all my heart and to be loved in return. I know what true love is. Nothing can take that away from me. My palm tree is gone but I enjoyed it for many years. Sometimes, all we have left are memories, and I'm choosing to be selective about mine. I'm remembering the good ones now.

# CHAPTER FOURTEEN
# BEYOND BELIEF

---

*Finding Connection in the Universe
and Ourselves*

*"The universe is not outside of you.
Look inside yourself; everything that
you want, you already are."*

Rumi

For most of my life I had believed in God. A judgmental almighty god in charge of everything. I don't believe that anymore but I do believe in a higher power, a creator, a source. I have found that believing in something outside of myself has been a comfort and a strength. I have concluded that it doesn't matter what you believe in, everyone seems to have different ideas, and that's ok, we all have the right to our own beliefs.

It amazes me that now I am not entirely sure of what the higher power consists of, I feel closer and more connected to it than ever. I feel it when I walk in the forest, when I touch my favourite tree and when I'm in my garden. I feel very connected when I sit in meditation and sometimes when I listen to a beautiful piece of music. Since I stopped believing in what I'd been told to believe and decided for myself what I wanted to think, what felt right I've become more mindful, and I notice more, and I think that's what connects me.

My intuition has always been good, but it's like a muscle: the more you use it, the stronger it gets. So now I use it all the time. I live my life by it. I don't second guess myself much anymore; I go with my first thought, and that is my connection. It's a connection to my higher self, to my subconscious. It's made me realise why I feel so good when I slow down and walk in the forest, when I take time to chat to the big fluffy black cat who comes to visit just when I need a bit of extra love, and why watching the birds on the feeder in my garden brings me this joy. It's because I am connecting with my truest self, the real me, the one I was too busy to know before.

I think that's all connection is really; it's slowing down so we can notice things, notice what's going on around us, instead of living the same life every day mindlessly because that's what we have always done. Once we slow down, everything changes. Gratitude becomes second nature because we notice more to be grateful for, and we see how amazing the small things are. We realise how much time we have for what's important, and we start to be more discerning about how we use our time. We become choosier about who we spend time with, in real life and in our virtual lives too. We do this because we have time to see instead of the constant hamster wheel of life we've been unthinkingly on.

Once we see the truth that we are all connected, everything in nature is connected, we feel less alone. It becomes easy to find comfort in nature, in a forest, in the garden or with an animal. The first sense we often use when we meet someone or see something for the first time is our eyes, our seeing sense. An animal uses energy, they sense your energy first. When we learn this fabulous skill that animals have naturally, it opens up a whole new world and we see more clearly.

This was brought home several years ago in a dramatic way. I was in France but had been bitten by a street dog in Bangkok a few months earlier. I had gone from never being afraid of an animal to fearing dogs, even small, adorable, gentle ones. I would shake and feel sick, and it took a few years for me to get over this. One day, I was out with my daughter and her friend. They both love animals, but my daughter's friend, Rose, has a special connection with them. We went past a house, and a dog came up to us. It came up to me and started to growl, and the hairs on the back of its neck stood up. I was terrified, and Rose saw this and called the dog over. It immediately went over to her, wagging its tale, and she petted it. Without me doing anything, the dog had sensed my fear and Rose's love.

Whether you believe in a god or gods, angels, spirit guides or anything else, the point is the connection. That knowing there is something deep within yourself that is part of everything else in the universe. I think that is a comfort on the dark days, to know you are not alone. That there is another part of you, a truer part, that always was and always will be.

Connection can be used as guidance, too, and a way to access our intuition. I sit in meditation every day, and because I am still and willing to listen and be guided, I am. I don't even know if it's a higher power, spirit guides, ancestors, angels, god or just another part of me, a higher version of me, but it doesn't matter. I'm comfortable not knowing and just having faith that there is something bigger than my physical human body guiding me if I choose to tap into it.

It's comforting to know we are not alone, and it explains a lot, especially when we take time to study nature. Even standing and watching a river is a connection to source. We can have connection in so many ways, but one of the easiest is when we are out in nature. Sometimes, I like to just stand still and listen and absorb. Meditation is another way. It's all about stillness, being mindful and slowing down, and this requires definite thinking about and even planning because it's so easy to just keep rushing from one thing to the next. What I do is I have definite times. I meditate every day for twenty to thirty minutes. When I walk in the forest, I make myself slow down and look at things.

The other connection that's important is connection with others. I've always been quite a loner and although I've had good friends over the years, my experiences have made me solitary, and I often isolate myself, which is not always healthy. There are times when it is important to be alone, and the ability to be happy on your own is a sign of strength, but it can turn into isolation if we are not careful. It can become a feeling of only wanting to rely on yourself and not trusting others. I learned important lessons around that which I talked about in the chapter on friends.

Connection with others enriches our lives not just in our personal life but in our work and business life too. We have not been designed to go it alone and to figure out everything on our own. We need other people. It took me many years to understand that. It all makes sense, though, when we realise that we are all connected, us, animals, nature, the creative source, everything. The sooner we all realise the importance of this, the better everything will be, socially and environmentally.

# CHAPTER FIFTEEN
# WORDS as ANCHORS

---

*The Transformative Power of Quotes
in Life's Storms*

*"The best word shakers were the ones
who understood the true power of
words. They were the ones who could
climb the highest."*

-Markus Zusak

I've always been a reader, a bookworm, so naturally, I love quotes. A few years ago, I started a business designing and selling art prints and mugs based on classic book quotes or quotes from authors. I didn't realise how much it meant to have these reminders around until I needed them.

When I came back to France after leaving my husband, the house that we'd shared was now mine, and I decorated it and added things without consulting anyone else as to their preferences. I realised that I would need constant positive reminders all around me, so I ordered some of my prints and other people's, too. I made myself mugs with quotes on to remind me of how I wanted to handle things.

One quote I found talked about going through a challenge with grace, bravery, courage and determination and as soon as I read it, I knew that's how I wanted to deal with the situation I found myself in. I made a mug with that quote on it so I could be reminded every morning as I drank my tea. I also put post-its on my fridge with those individual words on.

It's been proven that repetition forms new

habits and that we need to see things a certain number of times before it sinks into our subconscious. I figured that if I saw these reminders every day, multiple times a day, it would sink in and give me the strength I needed for what I had to do, which was rebuild my life or rather create a new one. I purposely chose quotes that embodied the qualities I wanted to display or quotes that inspired me to keep going. One of my favourites is the Albert Camus verse that talks about an invincible summer. "In the midst of winter, I found there was, within me, an invincible summer. And that makes me happy. For it says that no matter how hard the world pushes against me within me, there's something stronger – something better, pushing right back." It reminded me I may be in the darkest winter of my life, but I had strength inside I was learning to tap into.

Sometimes, it's only by looking back we can see how powerful and helpful something has been. This was one of those times. I did it by instinct. I've always been inspired by words, and I knew I needed a lot around me. When I was thinking of the things that helped me for this book, I remembered how the quotes and reminders around my house had strengthened me and reminded me not to give up and that things would improve.

Another empowering quote I found was from Haruki Murakami "And once the storm is over, you won't remember how you made it through, how you managed to survive. You won't even be sure whether the storm is really over. But one thing is certain. When you come out of the storm, you won't be the same person who walked in. That's what this storm's all about." I found it amazing that I came across so many quotes and pieces of writing that were just what I needed and exactly when I needed them. This was one of those quotes. I realised that I wanted to know the person who was going to walk out of that storm. I wanted to discover who I would become because this touched my heart. I knew I would be a different person. I had to be.

If you are a tea drinker like me or a coffee drinker, mugs are a great idea. Part of my website sells quote mugs, but it's also easy to find someone online who will custom-make a mug or two for you. Because the thing is, quotes are so very personal. What resonates so deeply with me may not be for you. But once you find a few that resonate, it's important to see them often, and that's why I like some of them on mugs. It's a gentle reminder, and eventually, it sinks in, and you stop one day and realise that you have put that quote into practice in your life.

So, where do you find quotes apart from reading them in books? I've used lots of methods. Social media sites like Instagram and Facebook. Pinterest is good. Google, which brings up written and picture types. You don't need to know the author, you can just google quotes about... being strong, being positive, not giving up, surviving etc. or an inspiring quote or motivating quote. You get the idea. Be warned, it can be addictive!

Quotes are great but they must be more than words. What I mean is we need to understand how to pull the meaning and wisdom from the quote. It's all well loving the words, but until we see how to use it in our lives it's just words on paper or a screen. So how do we do that? We stop, be still, and think instead of reading it and letting it wash over us. I like to put myself in the quote, make it very personal.

For example, with the Murakami quote I mentioned earlier, I knew I was in a storm, it felt exactly like that when I thought about it. If you've ever been in a strong storm, the feeling of being buffeted front, back and sideways by the wind, the driving rain in your face so you can't see, the loud thunder that makes you want to hide and the lightning that is terrifying. I've been in storms like this so when I read it, it resonated with me, and it felt like my life was at that moment. I also knew from the storms I'd been in, that they end. Either they stop or you find shelter. That feeling when the thunder and lightning stops and you don't know if it's over or if it will start again. If it's a powerful storm, there is that feeling of euphoria when you are safe because for a while you may have wondered if this was the time you really should have stayed home, that maybe you won't make it through this one. You've been through an experience, and like any experience, it changes you. I knew I was going through a huge experience, and I didn't know how or if I'd make it through, but one thing I was certain of, was that I wouldn't be the person I was before. I had to stop and take some time to contemplate the quote, to see how it fitted me and my circumstances. What could I get from it? What inspired me? How could I use it in my life at this moment?

Once you get into the habit of doing this, you will find you get a lot more from quotes and sayings that touch you in some way. All it takes is being still for a moment and asking yourself a few questions. It's worth it, don't you think? Once you've thought about it, it comes back to mind easily when you see the quote again. It's not a magic formula. It's part of the toolkit. That's why this book is called The Synergy Game. Life is a game we are playing, and our healing is not linear, one size fits all. It's little pieces all put together. A little help here, a little support there, and one day you look back and it's changed. I looked back and realised that my life was different. I had rebuilt my life. One thing did not do it, it was using all these things together so they became powerful, and I made huge changes more easily. It was like a holistic support system I had created for myself.

# CHAPTER SIXTEEN
# STYLED FOR MYSELF

---

*Embracing Self-Love Through the*
*Power of Personal Style*

*"Fashion is about dressing according to what's fashionable. Style is more about being yourself."*

Oscar de la Renta

You know that scene in *Eat Pray Love* when Julia Roberts is in a boutique with a friend, and she's looking at a beautiful sexy nightdress, and you can see she is sad because her marriage has ended, and she's thinking she has no one to wear it for? Her friend turns to her and says, 'Buy it for yourself', and she does because we see her in Italy in the apartment she's staying in, and she's bought herself some wonderful things to eat and is wearing the nightdress. For herself! Just to feel pretty and sexy and beautiful.

Don't underestimate the power of that. Of looking good for yourself. In the two years before I left my husband, I spent hours, countless effort and money in so many attempts to get him to notice me again. You see, he did used to. He used to tell me all the time that I was beautiful, he noticed what I wore or if I changed my hair. He would even notice if I bought a new lipstick. Then, suddenly, I became invisible. I thought it was because we had been together for so long, or that it was because I was becoming middle aged, entering my 50s, things were not as trim and perky as they once were! I thought it was that I was getting old. I felt unseen and unwanted. I bought new clothes, new underwear, changed my hair, and on and on.

When I left, I suddenly realised that I didn't have to worry any more about what he thought of what I was wearing or how my hair looked. I don't mean I didn't bother, I mean, for the first time in a long time, I was dressing for myself. I was looking in the mirror and liking what I saw, not wondering what he would think or wondering if he'd notice my new dress or that my hair and makeup looked good.

I saw myself properly, as just me. It was as if someone had turned the light on, and I could see clearly. I wasn't old and washed up. I still looked young for my age. My hair was nice, and my body wasn't bad at all, considering I was 53 and had given birth to two children. Incidentally, now, after over a year of yoga, I like it even more. I see how strong it is and I have an appreciation for it like I've never had before.

Once I could see myself clearly, and I only had myself to think about, and please, I started to experiment with clothes and buy things I hadn't before. For the first time, I wanted to look good for myself. To look in the mirror and say, yes, I like you, I like your hair, I like the clothes you've chosen today, and I like the way you've done your makeup.

It was important to feel good about the way I looked. When a marriage breaks up because of betrayal by one partner, the other partner is bound to question why and feel very lacking in self-confidence. What I realised, though, was that it was not me, it wasn't because I looked old or ugly. It was just something that happened. I knew it was important for my self-confidence to look after myself to be the best version of me I could be. Not to 'let myself go'. Plus, a great motivation was my two daughters. Right from the start, I wanted to show them what a strong woman is. How a strong woman acts, how she lives. How she rebuilds. This included looking after myself.

I've always loved clothes and shoes and everything girly. I've always loved nice underwear, although for a long time I bought it only to wear for my husband, not for myself. It was saved for special occasions. One sad day, when I was feeling sorry for myself and having a Netflix and sofa day, I happened to rewatch *Eat Pray Love* and saw that scene. I thought, why not? I can do that, too. I can buy things for myself, to make me feel good. It was like a revelation, something I'd never thought of doing before. I bought a beautiful set of lingerie in a pretty red. When I got home and tried it on, I felt good. Not because I was wearing it to impress someone else, to look sexy for a man. I felt good because I felt sexy, and it was all for me. To impress myself.

Without discussing any of this with my daughters as it wasn't really a conversation I wanted to have with them, my youngest brought me back the most wonderful gift on one of her UK trips. She had found a gorgeous vintage kimono in a shop in Oxford. She said she could imagine me wearing it, drinking my tea, and writing as I do in the mornings. It was perfect. It was in shades of salmon pink and red and went perfectly with a beautiful red silk nightdress I had bought. I copied Julia Roberts and wore them together, eating a delicious meal and sipping a glass of wine. I felt like Zelda Fitzgerald or Daisy Buchanan. I felt beautiful; I felt invincible. I don't think she ever realised how much that gift meant. It made me feel like a woman, and I looked at myself in the mirror and realised that I could do this. I could rebuild and be strong. I could actually have a life again.

I read a book a few years ago about colour therapy. It was interesting to learn what the different colours do for your moods and what it means when drawn to certain colours. For many years, I had dressed in dark colours. Always black underwear and mostly black and navy in my wardrobe, with some creams and greys thrown in for variety. Suddenly, I was drawn to bright colours. I bought a red jumper, then a green one. I bought a beautiful deep red dressing gown, but before I had stuck to black usually. It was as if my world was expanding via colour. I bought a pink t-shirt. I think it was the first pink thing I'd owned in many years! Spring arrived, and I bought a red dress and then a purple one. What was happening?

After not being seen for so long, suddenly, I wanted to be noticed. I wanted to feel confident. I didn't want to feel like I was someone to be pitied, someone that others feel sorry for. No, I wanted to be someone who people look at and think she looks good, she looks happy, she looks after herself. I found that looking my best, just for myself, lifted my mood. On days when I woke up with a heavy, sad feeling I started to 'dress up'. I would often choose a dress, beautiful matching underwear, put makeup on and do my hair. It didn't matter whether I was going out or having a day at home. It always made me feel better. To look in the mirror and like myself, helped me to change my mindset from "poor me, my husband cheated on me" to "what an idiot, look at what he's missing"! Now, at first, I must admit that saying things like that out loud to myself in the mirror made me wonder if I'd finally lost it completely. But like anything, if you hear it often enough, you believe it.

It's all part of falling in love with yourself. This realisation came late in life, and I wish so much I had been taught it earlier. The more I love myself, the more I have to give to others, and the more fully I can give of myself to others. It's self-care, self-respect, self-confidence and rebuilding myself. It's been part of finding out who I am. After being with, living with, someone else for so long. Being so close to someone, loving them, wanting to please them, I had lost myself along the way. I needed to be free to be me, but first, I had to find out who the hell me was!

I became the me I was so many years ago. But actually, that's not quite true. I became a truer version of me. Free of pleasing anyone, parents, partner or friends. Free of religious restrictions. For the first time in my life, it was all about me.

But that was just the beginning. I needed to

know myself a lot deeper than that. I needed to know what I wanted for the rest of my life, what my goals were and what my core values were now. Which led me to my next healing tool, study.

# CHAPTER SEVENTEEN
# LIFELONG LEARNER

---

*The Path of Self-Discovery Through Study*

*"Live as if you were to die tomorrow. Learn as if you were to live forever."*

Mahatma Gandhi

It seems a strange thing to include in a book about healing, but study and being a constant student is something that I've only seen the value of looking back. I realise that it's something I've always done but not seen as such a wonderful tool until now. Study helps us understand; it's the only way. I'm not talking about study for study's sake, just to gain knowledge. I'm talking about study that gets you closer to understanding yourself, to your passions and goals.

We cannot heal unless we get to know ourselves first. How could we? If we don't understand and know ourselves, we don't know what we need to heal or how to do it. However, getting to know ourselves intimately takes a huge amount of courage, and bravery and determination. It also takes honesty. If we can't be honest with ourselves about who we are, we cannot heal and grow.

There are many forms of study: self-study, guided study, study with a coach, reading, and watching videos. Anything that helps us grow and understand something is study. I am of the belief that we should be constantly learning and studying. It's a common misconception that learning stops when we leave school or college or university. That we have learned all we need to, all the basics for life. But how could that be when we are constantly changing and need to adapt? Our jobs and careers don't just stay static. If we run a business we need to be always thinking and learning how to improve it, how to be better, so why not ourselves too?

It amazing how the right things come to you exactly when you need them. When my marriage broke up, I was coming out of a thirty-three-year relationship and wasn't sure who I was anymore. If I wasn't a wife, if I didn't have a partner, who was I? An acquaintance emailed me one day and asked if she could pass my number on to a friend of hers who was travelling through Europe with his family. We are all involved with the same charity foundation, so I said yes. The family was not coming down to near where I live in France, they were staying in Paris, and after a few text messages back and forth, we had agreed to meet. Paris is a four hour train ride from me, so not a quick day trip, and it seemed like an illogical thing to do, but there was just something, a little voice inside urging me to go and meet this man. I didn't know why, I knew I needed to.

We met in a typical Parisian Cafe and sat and talked for five hours. It felt like I'd finally met someone who thought like me, who was on my wavelength. Everything he said made sense. For the previous six months I had been on autopilot, keeping the house and my business going, but I had lost a lot of motivation for the business that I had loved. I didn't know what I wanted for the rest of my life. I needed a new project, something to focus on that would light me on fire and renew my passion. The man I met with is a transformational life coach, helping people who want to get more out of their lives. He gave me a lot to think about, and his questions and our discussion had lit a spark that I wanted to feel more of. He offered me one of his courses, and although I said I'd think about it, I already knew what I would do and when he returned to Canada, we connected and set it up, and he's been my coach ever since.

To say it was life-altering is both dramatic and true. I thought in ways I never had before, to dig deep into myself was, at times, very uncomfortable but also very revealing. There were many aha moments, and a lot of the material was information I was familiar with, but having a coach made all the difference. I was accountable to someone, and I had someone to bounce things off, share achievements and get a much deeper understanding than if I'd just self-studied as I had in the past.

It was a six-month course, and at the beginning, you are required to set a goal, a big one. I set one, but within three months, it had changed so that there was nothing familiar about it, and it was scary. The reason it changed so much was that I was learning for the first time in my life about myself and my wants and needs, who I wanted to be and what I wanted to do. I had never thought so deeply about it before, but now I knew that I wanted to use my experiences in life and how I'd overcome challenges to help others do the same thing. There was nothing special about me. I didn't have a privileged upbringing, and I wasn't well connected. I felt as if people could relate. If I could rebuild my life, create the life I wanted to live, wouldn't it be wonderful if I could help others do the same?

It felt right, and my passion was back. There was no way I would have discovered this if I hadn't taken the time to get to know myself through the study course. Once I had decided, all sorts of information came to me, other learning I needed to do to get me closer to my goal. I knew I could write a book. I had been writing since I was a child, but I had no idea of how to market and publish a book. But in the serendipitous way of the universe, I came across the perfect course for what I needed.

Every bit we learn, every morsel we study, should be for a specific purpose and not just for acquiring knowledge. Once we know ourselves and our needs, we may find we want to go further in a specific area. This happened a few years ago when I saw an energy healer. She used crystals, and I was fascinated. This also led me to study reiki and other healing modalities. It was perfect timing as I needed the healing, and it helped me to let go of some past hurts and limiting beliefs. I used it to help others, too. It's something that I will always have no matter what I do in life. I still use all I've learned. I wear specific crystals every day, I do self-reiki and use crystal grids around my home and I use sound healing. Although I am a reiki and crystal practitioner on paper, I don't practice apart from on myself anymore or for friends. But when I studied it, I had a specific purpose in mind. A few years later my plans changed, my life changed, and I went in a different direction, but I'm so glad I took the opportunity when it presented itself.

I know I'll always be learning and studying

myself. My needs will change as my life changes. I know that without a doubt the more I study myself the better person I become. The better person I become the richer my life is in every way.

# CHAPTER EIGHTEEN
# VIBRATIONAL HEALING

---

*Harnessing Energy for Balance and Renewal*

*"Everything in life is vibration."*

Albert Einstein

As I mentioned in the previous chapter, energy healing made a huge difference. Like anything holistic it's not a magic wand, a one-session and your cured type of thing. But neither is it harmful. What it did for me was give me added strength and balance. When I felt like I couldn't cope, an energy healing session or a reiki session would sort of even me out again, like taking a deep breath and with effects lasting for days, sometimes weeks, and over time, helping me cope with and get rid of deep-seated issues.

The concept of healing is vast and covers everything from open heart surgery to herbalism, from a hot lemon and honey drink when you have a cold to a plaster cast when you've broken your leg. (At least that's what I had when I broke mine!) Energy healing is also a modality with many options, and it's easy to find one you resonate with. For me, it was particularly crystals, reiki and aromatherapy, but there are also massage, sound healing, acupuncture, homeopathy, reflexology, qigong, and quantum energy healing, and so many more. I've tried quite a few of these, and I'd encourage you to try as many as possible to see which resonates most with you.

The first time I went to see an energy healer

of the sort that could be thought of as 'woo woo' was after I had left the religion that I had been a part of for most of my life. I was forty-nine at the time and knew I had a crazy amount of limiting beliefs I needed help with, not only from following strict rules all my life but also from a rigid and rule-orientated upbringing. I needed to go from being taught that it was selfish to put myself first, that anything that can't be explained is from the devil, and that the world was ending soon. Just a few little things I no longer believed in my head, but my subconscious hadn't caught up.

The lady I went to see had been practicing for many years and used a combination of massage, sound healing, crystals, colour therapy and infrared therapy. Whatever she felt you needed she used, and it was different every time. It was my first introduction to the world of crystals and almost everything else she used, too. She worked completely with her intuition and used a pendulum to find out what I needed, what vitamins I lacked and when I should come back for another visit. A whole new world had opened up to me, and once I felt the benefits of it, better sleep and less anxiety, I wanted to learn more about how it all worked. I wanted to understand why this was making a difference.

I bought a few books. That's usually my first port of call when I want to learn something. I started reading about energy healing and why it is so effective. The more I learned, the more it all made sense. It's all about vibration. We are vibrating. Everything in the universe is vibrating. If our vibration is off or low, no wonder we feel awful. Energy healing is all about balancing everything: our four bodies, physical, emotional, mental and spiritual. The more I learned, the more I wondered how I was still functioning, as there seemed so much that was out of balance.

Nature is amazing and is so fabulous at healing itself once the irritants, pollutants and harmful influences are taken away. I grew up in the north of the UK, in Wales, and our nearest city was Liverpool, so we used to visit a few times a year. The river that runs through the city is called the River Mersey, and it was notorious for being filthy and polluted. People used to say you couldn't drown in the Mersey; you'd die of poisoning first. In the 1980s, it started to change as measures were put into practice to clean it up. It was a huge undertaking costing over £300 million, and it didn't happen overnight. Slowly, over the next couple of decades, things started to improve, and all they had done was stop the raw sewage pollution from going in the river anymore. The rest was done by nature as the river cleaned itself and wildlife returned.

It's like that with us. Sometimes, we need to get rid of toxic things in our life, things polluting our environment, thoughts and feelings. It could be anything from having a bad diet to being around toxic people. For me, it was toxic thoughts and people. I needed to change my thinking drastically. I had been brought up to believe anyone who wasn't part of the same faith was bad and not to be associated with, that I was an imperfect sinner who was only alive on earth because of God's undeserved kindness, and that the world would end soon. This was so damaging I now realise. To constantly be dwelling on negative things, to be constantly reminded that you are imperfect and a sinner, is so wrong.

Like the river Mersey, once I left all that behind, I changed my thinking. However, I needed help. The money spent on the Mersey was for a huge purpose-built treatment plant so the sewage pollution wouldn't go in the river anymore. That was to help the river so it could heal itself. My 'treatment plant' was to visit an energy healer who helped me release a lot of the negativity that had built up over the years so that my body and mind could heal and regenerate and think in the way I was designed to think, positively. I gradually changed beliefs about myself and let go of trauma I had been carrying since childhood. My mother's decision to cut off contact with me, although painful became a blessing as I saw how her toxic beliefs and judgmental attitude affected me.

Energy healing isn't like waving a magic wand, but it can have instant effects. Sometimes, I would go in with awful neck or shoulder pain from the stress I was carrying, and after the massage and infrared therapy, I'd walk out pain-free. The thought changes and limiting beliefs I wanted to let go of took longer and more work, and not just using energy healing. I used many of the other tools I've spoken about in this book. When I first used to visit her, I would feel guilty thinking what I was doing was so wrong, expecting to become possessed with demons like I'd been taught. Funnily enough, that never happened.

I view my energy healing tools as my supportive friends. It's a part of my life to have regular reiki sessions, to use crystals in my home and on myself as jewellery, and to use aromatherapy oils to raise the vibration of my space, to energise, calm to comfort. Whatever is needed.

What I've learned is that energy healing is not like taking an aspirin for a headache, and within a few minutes, the pain has gone. It's more like a support that, when used along with other things like a healthy diet and regular exercise, things that are well within our control, can help situations we have lost control of like our sleep patterns, our daily balance and harmony. It literally raises our vibration and our mood and outlook. A higher vibration is a more positive state to be in. It's impossible to sustain this 24/7 but it's good to be aware of how our body is at any one time. We do this by constantly checking our thoughts and tuning in to how we feel.

At first, this seems like a lot of work, constantly having to track ourselves, but after a while, it becomes routine, and you raise your vibration. For me, it's music or going for a walk in nature or dancing around my living room. Often, it's writing, getting lost in words and creating. For you, it could be reading a book, watching TV, chatting to your best friend, or cooking a meal. Everyone is different, and once we find these tools that can change our state, it's better than winning the lottery because we have discovered something that is key to our happiness, and that is priceless.

# CHAPTER NINETEEN
# CREATING MY SANCTUARY

---

*The Art of Personalising Space for Healing*

*"Let your home be your masterpiece and let it reflect your deepest values and desires. In its comfort, find your peace."*

– Georgia Clare

What you see every day, your surroundings, affects your mood and your energy. If everything is chaos, then your mind will feel it, and there will be no free-flowing energy. I'm not saying you have to be a neat freak, I'm definitely not that. I do like order, though, and putting things back where they belong. But this is not what I'm talking about when I say that 'my space' is one of the things that helped me.

Making what was once our home into my home was healing. I found out what I liked and made it my own space. But I also filled it with 'feel good' things. It was winter, so I bought a heated blanket. I bought cushions in bright colours and lots of plants. I spread my crystals around and burned incense. I made it so that my house was my safe place, somewhere I looked forward to coming back to. I filled the walls with art. Pieces that inspired me or brought me joy when I looked at them.

But I also used the fact that now I was living alone to do things like pin affirmations to the fridge and hang my favourite quotes on the walls. I bought prints of poems that inspired me and framed them. As I've already mentioned, I made mugs with quotes that were inspiring so that every day, as I drink my tea, I can be reminded of how I want to be.

I made my home pretty and cosy. It was winter and my first winter in Europe for many years and I knew if I was to survive it, I would need more than warm clothes. At this point, my house was only two-thirds renovated and the next big job was new windows, as although the old ones looked good, they were draughty, and the glass was thin. Along with the heated blanket, I bought cosy bedding and cosy cushions for my bed. None of these things were expensive, but it made it more my own place, and more important it made me happy when I looked around me.

I knew I had a lot of work to do to get the house finished, apart from the windows. My husband had always been a practical guy, so we didn't ever hire workmen to do things, he did it all himself. I had no idea how to find people to do the work, but I also realised that I could actually learn to do some of the work myself. So, I did something I haven't done before, I asked for help. I don't mean to get the jobs done for free, but for recommendations and for friends to show me how to do things. I'm fortunate as I have a capable girlfriend who does many DIY jobs herself and another who's partner is a builder.

I had inherited many tools from my husband, so one day in the autumn my patio and the front area of the house were dirty and needed pressure washing. I had seen one in the cellar but had no idea how to use it, so I asked my DIY friend, and she came over and showed me what to do. It's hard to describe the feeling of satisfaction as I saw how good I was making it all look. I was so proud of myself.

My next job to tackle was some decorating. I knew how to do it in theory but had only done it under the supervision of my husband. I hadn't decided on style or colours, we always discussed it together or he decided. I turned an unrenovated room upstairs into a guest room. I'd never had a guest room. For years, when my girls were at home, it was just their rooms and ours. An extra room for guests seemed like a luxury, and the house was never big enough, but now it was. I had three bedrooms, and I only needed one to sleep in. I ventured into the cellar and found paint, brushes and a sander. It had been plasterboarded but needed sanding before I could paint. I knew that much! Who knew that a little machine could make so much dust! I took a day to sand it and a day to clean up the mess.

The freeing thing was that I had no rules about how it should be. It was my house now, and I could do it any way I liked. It didn't need to be perfect. I bought Matthew McConaughey's book Greenlights on Audible, put my headphones on and got to work. It was summer, so I had all the windows open, and as the paint started to cover the walls, a feeling came over me that this was mine. That I was caring for and improving my own house. I had never had a house all to myself before. I think that's when I fell in love with it. It had kept me safe, and now I repaid that by making it look pretty and fixing it. The satisfaction and pride I felt when I had finished that room, put the newly painted bed back together, and the bedside tables I had painted a lovely cream shade on either side with their new lamps on is hard to put into words. My daughter was coming to stay, and her genuine praise lifted me even higher.

Making my space nice meant effort, but the satisfaction and pleasure I got out of it was so worth it. Lighting candles at night and putting on pretty lights, watering my ever-growing collection of plants, buying myself flowers and getting rid of a few things I didn't like. When you live with another person, actually three other people, for a while, as the girls lived there with us for a few years, you collect a lot of stuff not necessarily to your taste. At least, that's my experience. I took time to go through each room in the house and ask myself whether I actually liked the things in it, and if I didn't, they were sold or given away or moved down to the cellar.

The more I decorated and rearranged and added things I liked, the more it became my own space. It became my sanctuary and my safe place. It became a place where I could relax and start to build myself a new life. I've made it peaceful and calm. The energy in it is all mine, so I can control how it feels. I can make sure that it's all good positive energy, and if needed, I can go around the house releasing any negative energy because I am aware of how it should feel. I use sage and incense for this, making sure that it is ethically sourced and produced. Sometimes I use essential oils and I also use sound. Tingshas and wind chimes and also music. These are all things I have learned work effectively to raise the vibration of the space I am in.

I knew that I needed my space to be clean in every way, physically and energetically. I knew that I needed to look at nice things to elevate my mood and spirit. I still feel like that. I'm definitely not overly house-proud, I like to feel I live here and am not just a guest. But surroundings are important to our mood. Even just small changes can make a difference. A plant, some flowers, a new brightly coloured cushion cover or some candles can make all the difference.

# CHAPTER TWENTY
# REWRITING MY NARRATIVE

---

*The Journey of Changing Our Story*

*"The only person you are destined to become is the person you decide to be."*

Ralph Waldo Emerson

We all have stories we tell ourselves; some are empowering, and some take our power away. I realised a few years ago that I could change my story. When faced with a challenge and life has not turned out the way we planned or thought it would, we have two choices. We can either take responsibility and take charge of our life or we can shift the blame onto others and give them the power over our life and future.

Bad things happen, things change, people change, and we don't always get the happy ending we planned. It's how we deal with the changes in our life that determine our future. We tell ourselves stories, and we tell others our stories. We do it without thinking. For most of my life I found it very challenging to find my way around in new places. I told myself I had a terrible sense of direction and often got lost. This was not great in my job as a photographer, where often I had to go to new places and find my way around cities I'd never been to.

I read about this concept of changing my story and decided to apply it to this. I started to tell myself that I would make good choices when navigating and that I could easily find my way. The amazing thing is that I didn't get lost so much, and I didn't get so stressed about it all. I just changed the story I was telling myself. Now, it's not like magic. It takes effort. I had to remind myself constantly, and I had to be aware of my thinking all the time so that when I had a thought of, "Oh no, how am I going to get there?" I had to change the wording to, "No problem, I have my phone. I'll easily find my way".

Being aware of thoughts all the time can show us where we need to make changes. It is very hard to do, as a lot of our stories have been told to us by our parents and are in our DNA. This can all be changed. It must be changed as it can affect not just our mental and emotional health but even our physical health.

As my mother got older, she started to develop arthritis in her hands. She wasn't surprised, she accepted it, almost even expected it. Why? Because my grandfather, her father, suffered from arthritis. She said once that she was like her father, so that's why she had it. She had inherited it. The study of epigenetics has shown that much more is at play than originally thought, that environment and experiences play a big role in our physical state. The story my mother told herself was not necessarily true, but she believed it.

The stories that we tell other people are how

we perceive ourselves. If the story we are telling is one of victimhood, of always being badly done to, of hardship and sadness, there is no room for change. We will only get more of the same. "Thoughts become things" is not just a clever saying, it's actually true.

Years ago, I had a friend who was dynamic and sociable, loved to party and have fun, but was always falling out with people and being disappointed in others. Her life was filled with drama. As I got to know her, I found out this was her story. Her childhood had been traumatic, with abuse and abandonment by her mother when she was just twelve years old, leaving her with the abuser. But this defined her, this was her story, her reason for drinking a lot and partying too much and always being disappointed by people. In reality, she was unhappy with herself, always trying to escape, but underneath, she was a frightened little girl who could trust no one. She needed to change her story.

It is much easier to stay with the story we tell ourselves rather than craft a new one. New things can be scary; the unknown can be terrifying. Stepping into the unknown takes a huge amount of courage, bravery and faith. But we can do it in small steps.

Obviously, it can be the case that our external story changes without us being in control. However, our inside story is always in our control. It's what we tell ourselves, and we have to watch what we tell ourselves.

In my case, I've changed my story a few times in my life. I came from an abusive childhood, and when I was twenty-nine, I 'outed' my father as an abuser, the consequences of which sent him to prison. That was me changing my story from being a quiet and obedient daughter to taking control of my story. Was it scary? Terrifying! But for the first time in my life, I felt powerful and in control. My story changed from victim to survivor and someone taking charge of her life. I wasn't just letting things go on around me anymore. I was changing the narrative.

I became someone who made things happen. Actually, I had always been like that, but not consciously. Now, I was aware of what I could do if I took control of my story. I've become a few different things since then. I became a photographer long before I actually felt like one. The saying 'fake it till you make it' is actually better lived as 'fake it till you become it'. I didn't feel like the successful photographer my husband told everyone I was (he exaggerated!) for quite a while. It took a lot of successful jobs and buying better and better equipment until I finally was proud of what I did and felt genuine when I told people what I did. But living it long before I could say to people I was a photographer, ensured that I became it. You see in my heart I knew I was, I just doubted myself every now and then.

That's a practical way of changing your story, but it's been a lot of use in my healing journey, too. When I found out my husband had cheated on me, after the initial shock had subsided somewhat, a little voice, actually, it was a rather loud shouting voice, inside me said YOU WILL NOT BE A VICTIM!! On no, hell no, fuck no! I wasn't going to play the poor cheated-on wife for others to feel sorry for, someone who my girls and sister worried about, and someone who was so brokenhearted that it defined her for the rest of her life.

Now anything that devastates us changes us, but it didn't have to define me. There's a huge difference. If I let it define me, I am being controlled by what happened. I am letting the situation dictate the rest of my life. If I let it change me, I was in control. I could control the changes and decide how

I wanted to be changed. I could create a new story for myself. With such a huge life change, my friends and family felt sorry for me and were devastated at what had happened, but going forward, it was me who could shape how I was treated and perceived. Were they going to see me as a sad, abandoned woman or a woman who could rise again like a phoenix? It was up to me to decide how I wanted to be seen and to make it happen.

I changed my story from being a woman who was a wife and cared for and who never needed to take care of house and car maintenance, never drove on long journeys, never had to fix anything and was complacent about the future. I became a woman who could take the car to the garage and knew how to check the oil and tire pressure. I became a woman who could do small house repairs and decorating, who could order wood for the winter and stack it all on her own, who could buy a new lawnmower and strimmer and take care of the garden, who could hire workmen to do the work she couldn't, who could drive up to her sister's five hours away all by herself. I became a woman who decided for herself what was right for her because, for the first time in her life, she was choosing herself. And I became a woman who was happy again and so very proud of her achievements. A woman probably for the first time in her life, standing by herself with no backup and being ok with it. I became a strong woman. Maybe I always had been, but now this was my story, it was who I was, who I am.

# CHAPTER TWENTY-ONE
# THROUGH THE LENS

---

*Healing and Self-Discovery with Photography*

*"Photography is a way of feeling, of touching, of loving. What you have caught on film is captured forever... It remembers little things, long after you have forgotten everything."*

Aaron Siskind

Photography became what journaling was and had been. It became a record of my progress and a visual diary. I have been a photographer since around 2010, it's been my business, but I never thought of using it as a healing tool. I realised, though, that I could turn it into something that would help me not just to pay my bills which it was already doing, but it could help me in my healing.

The first way was an obvious way, and one thing that drew me to photography many years ago, and that was that it made me more mindful. It made me stop and notice things and took my mind off any pain and sadness I was feeling. It wasn't permanent, but those focused moments when I was composing a shot or looking for something to take a photo of meant that my mind was at peace, and I was absorbed in doing something I loved. I took my phone with me every time I went for a walk in the forest to document the changing seasons and scenery. It was a little project that meant that instead of wandering through the forest on my walks with no purpose, I started to notice things I hadn't before. I took new paths and felt more like exploring. I took a ridiculous number of photos of the beautiful moss on the trees deep in the forest. I found new ways of capturing the river and the waterfall. I tried a lot of close-ups of leaves and branches.

Sometimes, when I didn't feel like going out, the thought of photos I may miss taking got me out there. Some photos I edited, and some stayed on my phone. It doesn't matter where you are in the world, whether you live in a city or a village or in the middle of nowhere, you can always see your world in more detail. We rush so many things, even a beautiful forest walk. There's always something to do, something to get back for, so this was helping me to slow down and be much more mindful.

The second way I used my photography was selfies. I had never been a big fan. As a photographer, I was usually behind the lens and didn't particularly like having my photo taken. The thing is with selfies, though, is that they are for you. There is no need to do anything with them. I took them on sad days, and on happy days, and every day between. I took them when I'd been crying and looked terrible and when I'd was all dressed up and going out.

One day I had the idea of trying to capture what I was feeling with my camera. It was in the summer, so the weather was warm. I decided that I felt stripped of all that was familiar, so I took off my top and just sat there in front of the camera in my skirt. I brought up all the emotions I was feeling: the pain, the hurt, the anger, the utter devastation. I sat on a chair; then I curled up on the floor. I gripped the back of the chair, and I gazed into the camera with tears pouring down my face, my mouth open in a silent scream for how helpless I felt. I'm not sure how long I spent doing it, but when I'd finished, I felt lighter. I felt like I had let go of some of my emotions that were overwhelming. I still have those photographs. I would delete them, but I thought they would be a good reminder for me of how far I had come. So that when I'm having a sad day, nothing will ever feel so bad again.

My selfies also chronicled my bodily changes with my yoga practice. I could see how much firmer I was looking. It's amazing how much we forget, and that is why it's so important to look back and see. And finally, my selfies showed me I still looked good. I wasn't a washed-up middle-aged old woman who no one would ever want. I wasn't as ugly and wrinkled and awful as I was feeling. I was ok and I was happy with myself. My selfies helped restore my self-confidence.

Not exactly photography, but another thing I used was video selfies. At first, I used them like a letter. I spoke to my husband as if he was there. I told him how I was feeling. I told him what was going on in my life, what I'd been doing, what I'd accomplished. Now that *really* helped. To go from living with someone for so long to nothing, no contact, was hard to accept and get used to. So, by making these videos, I was weaning myself off him. In a way, I still talked to him and told him things, and again it got it out of my head. It helped that I offloaded the hurt and the pain I was feeling into these videos. We were on opposite sides of the world, so it wasn't like I could tell him how I was feeling face to face. As with writing it all down and getting it out, saying it on video, let it out of me, so all these feelings weren't trapped inside. I always felt drained but lighter after pouring my heart into a video. It's very important to find these outlets for our emotions; it's definitely not good to keep them bottled up inside.

Some days, I would do a video diary sort of thing to document how and what I was feeling. It became so helpful in the coming months as I looked back and saw how far I had progressed. When I watched a video from two or three months previously, I could see that although maybe I didn't feel as if I was progressing, I actually was. It was like reading my journal entries, I could see that, little by little, I was healing and building a life for myself.

Documenting my life with photography and videos has been quite an eye-opener for me because it made me realise that I forget things. I suppose that's the whole reason for family snapshots and holiday photos. Because we don't always remember how good it was until it's gone. For a long time, I wasn't able to look at our family pictures, it made me too sad to think that we were no longer the four of us. But now I can look at them and remember all the good times, all the fun we had and all the adventures. I can remember through the photos what a good father and provider he was, instead of remembering the hurt and pain and when it all went wrong. My photos help me to see that I was loved at one time, that I had something very special that many people go their whole lives without finding, and I'm so grateful for that. I had a beautiful love story. It ended but that's ok because not all love stories are meant to last forever. Sometimes, we are meant to take different paths.

I look at my photography hanging on the walls of my home, and it reminds me of places we visited together. A photograph is a moment in time captured no matter what the subject is. My moments are hanging on my walls, and as I look around me, I can see the first time we went to Cambodia as a family, a fabulous beach day we had on the west coast of France and that time we walked the back streets of Bangkok. No matter what has happened these photos remind me I have so many happy memories and that they far outweigh the sad ones. I choose to keep the happy ones and let the sad ones go. But you need not be a photographer to do all this. The video and photo selfies I took to remind me are not all professional. Many photos I look back on are just snapshots. It's what is in the photos healing. A reminder of how far I've come and how rich my life has been with love.

# CHAPTER TWENTY-TWO
# FALLING IN LOVE WITH ME

*Synergy of Self-Love*

*"To fall in love with yourself is the first secret to happiness."*

Robert Morley

The title of this chapter sounds narcissistic, but it's not. One of the most important things I've discovered on my healing journey (actually, I'd say that it's the most important) is how important it is to love myself if I am to heal and live my best life.

If I can't love myself, then I'm not really in a position to love anyone else fully. I need to fill my cup first before I can share the contents with anyone else, otherwise I am trying to give from an empty cup. If I give from a cup that is not full, that is low, then it will soon be empty and depleted like my energy and my vitality.

So, what does it mean to love myself? Spa days and new shoes have their place, and I love them both, but that's not what I'm talking about. I've learned a lot about myself recently, I've had more time to think and to study myself. To live my best life and to be my best self I needed to do both of these things a lot. It seems very self-centred to say that I've made a study of myself and continue to do so, but that was the only way I would find out what I needed, what I wanted and what I liked. We are all told so early in life what we need and what we want without actually being taught to think for ourselves. It's the way things usually are. We often go along with what our parents want, then what our school friends think and then our partners, co-workers, and peers. How many times do we actually stop and take the time to study what we actually want away from anyone else's expectations or opinions?

It takes absolute honesty with ourselves, and sometimes it's not what we want to see. We are revealing our true selves to ourselves. Not seeing the self that we want others to see, but the real you, the real me. It takes courage and bravery because once we see our true selves it's all on us. We realise everything is our responsibility, and we can blame no one else anymore.

It sounds scary, and it is, but the benefits are immeasurable. Knowing myself and what I need has made me a better person, a better mother, sister and friend. Because I'm me. I'm not someone else's version of what they want me to be. I realised that I was like this for years. I tried to be who I thought my parents wanted me to be then I tried to be who I thought my husband wanted me to be. The most wonderful thing I've realised, though, is that if I am just me and people like me for that, there is no better feeling in the world. Then, I can relax and enjoy being with my friend who loves me for being my true self. The people who you don't resonate with anymore will naturally drift away or maybe even run away! But you will find that that's ok; it may give you momentary disappointment, but loving yourself means you soon realise that you didn't vibe anymore and that you are probably better off without each other.

Everything I've written in this book has helped me to fall in love with myself. When my marriage broke up, I realised something profound. I had been relying on other people to love me all my life, and many had shown me I was not really worth loving as myself. I became an option and a backup plan for my husband. I wasn't quite the daughter my mother wanted, and I was an object for my father to play with for his enjoyment. So, I decided to love myself the way I wanted others to love me.

I took better care of my health. I had always eaten healthily, but now I stepped it up and made it a priority. I was never very good at sticking to any exercise routine, but now I realised that it would be essential to my life. I started learning yoga with my friend, and once I'd learned enough, I committed to practising five days a week. I started saying no to things I previously would have agreed to just because I never wanted to let anyone down or disappoint them. I started making sure I wasn't disappointing myself instead. I made a determined effort to get my sleep pattern back on track, as I knew that was vitally important.

I started thinking. Not just regular thinking but deep contemplative thinking along with writing. I needed to find out what I wanted out of life from now on. In a way, my life had been on autopilot. Got married, had children, earned money, kept house, but all that had now changed, and my children had grown up, and I was single. For the first time in my life, there was only me to think about. What was I going to do with the rest of my life? I had no idea. For a while, it had been about surviving and acceptance, coming to terms with the huge life change, but now the dust had settled I needed a plan, a life plan.

As I mentioned in the chapter on study, I met my coach at exactly the right time. It was as if the universe knew what I needed and was making sure everything fell into place for the next stage of my journey. The program I started studying was exactly what I needed. I thought I was a thinker! But this made me dig deeper into myself than I even realised was possible. It changed my thinking completely and helped me to realise that what I thought I wanted for my life at the beginning of the course wasn't what I wanted by the time I had finished it.

I had a plan. I had no idea how I would make it happen, but I had a plan. I had achieved so much I wanted to. I had overcome childhood trauma, left behind limiting beliefs from a lifetime of being part of a strict religion, and I had made peace with the breakup of my marriage. I will always be a work in progress. There will always be more layers to peel back and heal. That's just life, but I was happy, and once again, my life had a why, a reason to get up in the morning and goals to work towards.

I realised one day that not only did I love my life, but I had fallen in love with myself. I was no longer looking to others for validation or commendation.

I was secure in who I had become. I think when you survive your worst nightmare, the most awful thing, you see your strengths. To look back on what you have done is a wonderful thing to do. Society tells us we should be small and humble and not brag about what we've done. Now, obviously, a person who does that constantly is obnoxious to be around, but we need to be that person around ourselves. We need to give ourselves commendation all the time for what we achieve, even if it's a small win, and around others, we can own what we've done and not dismiss or diminish ourselves. When someone compliments us on an achievement or how we look, how do we react? The correct way to act is to say thank you and accept the compliment. Often, we don't. We dismiss it so we can make ourselves smaller and more acceptable.

I can't put this any better than Marianne Williamson in her book *Return to Love* where she said, "Our deepest fear is not that we are inadequate. Our deepest fear is that we are powerful beyond measure. It is our light, not our darkness that most frightens us. We ask ourselves, 'Who am I to be brilliant, gorgeous, talented, fabulous?' Actually, who are you not to be? You are a child of God. Your playing small does not serve the world. There is nothing enlightened about shrinking so that other people won't feel insecure around you. We are all meant to shine, as children do. We were born to make manifest the glory of God that is within us. It's not just in some of us; it's in everyone. And as we let our own light shine, we unconsciously give other people permission to do the same. As we are liberated from our own fear, our presence automatically liberates others."

I wasn't playing small anymore. No more hiding my achievements so others wouldn't feel uncomfortable. I realised that was not the right way to think. If I made them feel uncomfortable, that was not anything to do with me; that was them, and even better, I may be a source of inspiration. Other people had inspired me with their accomplishments, so maybe I could do that, be that person who inspired.

Thanks to yoga, walking and a healthy diet, I am strong and healthy. Thanks to my journalling, gratitude practice and meditation, my mind is more at peace. Thanks to music and dance, my friends and the beautiful space I have created for myself, I am happy. Thanks to many of the other practices and tools I've used I've been able to let go of much of the pain and sadness in my life so I live a full life. I realised long ago that I couldn't live a full life if I carried all these emotions with me.

What I really hope is that some of what I've spoken about here can help you. I'm an ordinary person who has been fortunate enough to come across these healing tools. They've made a difference in my life and allowed me to move on, let go and live a fabulous life rich in every way. I live in a beautiful home in the south west of France and am blessed with friends and neighbours I love. Every day, I get to do what I love for work: writing and sharing what I have learned. I can't think of a better way of life. I made this life. I created it, and you can too. If I can do it, anyone can. It takes one thing, and it was the one thing that JFK used to send a rocket to the moon and that the Wright brothers used to build an aeroplane. It's simply the will to do it.

# KEEP THE JOURNEY GOING...

Thank you for being a part of The Synergy Game. This book is just the beginning of our journey together, and if you've found the ideas and practices here helpful, I'd love to invite you to explore more through my website. Over at georgiaclare.com, you'll find deeper insights, guided tools, and additional resources that mirror the concepts in this book—only there, we go even further.

The website is an extension of The Synergy Game, designed to help you apply these ideas to your everyday life with more clarity. I offer a variety of courses that dive into everything from meditation and mindset work to mastering self-love and creating lasting personal change. These are designed to empower you with practical, actionable steps that align with your goals.

I also host a meditation podcast (https://georgiaclare.substack.com/podcast) where we explore guided meditations to bring more peace and balance to your life. Whether you're new to meditation or looking to deepen your practice, the podcast is a gentle companion to your self-discovery journey.

Don't forget to subscribe to my newsletter (https://therebuildcompass.com), where I share more inspiration, tools, and fresh ideas. It's a weekly nudge to keep you moving forward, bringing together everything we talk about in the book, but with real-life applications and encouragement to stay on track.

I've created these additional resources because I believe in the power of synergy—that when we combine the right tools with consistent action, incredible things happen. I'd love for you to explore, connect, and keep building the life you want to live. You don't have to do it alone, and there's a whole community waiting for you.

Looking forward to seeing you there.

With gratitude,
Georgia Clare

# ABOUT THE AUTHOR

Georgia is a writer, photographer, and seeker of truth whose life's journey navigates through vibrant landscapes of self-discovery and transformation. Born near the vibrant city of Liverpool and raised amidst the scenic beauty of North Wales, her path has been anything but ordinary. Embarking on life within the confines of a strict religious upbringing and a childhood marked by abuse, Georgia's midlife pivot was not merely a departure from a tightly knit community but a profound exploration of self, healing, and empowerment following the end of a decades-long marriage. This shift marked a courageous step towards a more authentic and fulfilling existence.

Writing and photography, Georgia's twin passions, have served as conduits for her voice and vision. Through her poignant words, she delves into resilience, personal growth, and the restorative power of self-love, while her photography captures fleeting moments of beauty and transformation, mirroring her own journey of rebirth. The concept of synergy— the notion that the whole is greater than the sum of its parts—has been a cornerstone of Georgia's path to wellness. By weaving together practices such as meditation, yoga, gratitude, and the profound impact of quotes, she has embraced a holistic approach to healing that resonates with and inspires others on their paths to well-being.

Today, Georgia flourishes, committed to sharing the insights gleaned from her journey. Through her work, she aspires to empower others to face their own trials, embrace their authentic selves, and discover joy in the synergy of life's offerings. Residing in the serene Southwest of France, the surrounding beauty continues to fuel her journey and creative expression.

www.ingramcontent.com/pod-product-compliance
Lightning Source LLC
LaVergne TN
LVHW040008200726
843493LV00005B/1178